GHOST TOWN
EL DORADO

GHOST TOWN
EL DORADO

BY

LAMBERT FLORIN

TWIN BUTTES BUILDING, purpose unknown, photographed through wire barrier. Town is near highway, worth trip to discover if owners have changed minds about allowing access to historic camp.

Bonanza Books • New York

FOREWORD

The men who settled the old West came from all walks of life, from New England states, the old South, the Midwest, from Canada, Mexico and from across the seas. Originally trained as farmers, artisans, professional men or without preparation of any kind, most adapted themselves to a new, and generally rigorous life. When their settlements came to a premature end they refused to admit defeat or return to their homes. They moved on to greener pastures and tried again for success. Most eventually left their bones beneath the sod of western prairies or tall timber of coastal ranges or continental divide.

The first women to join these adventurers were a softly curved, hard eyed lot. They were camp followers as were those who trailed after the legions of Rome. They were out for personal gain, reaped from the need of men for female companionship, however sordid.

In a few years when a man had accumulated sufficient worldly goods to support a mate, he "sent back home" for a childhood sweetheart. On arrival in the rough mining camp or cattle town the intended bride was likely to be dismayed, and some got back on the stage to return home. But most stayed to begin a new life. These women are among the most courageous in history, enduring loneliness, deprivation of the society of their own kind and a complete lack of the accustomed conveniences of their former life "back East."

Many of these early day settlements in the West were based on one industry, the mining of precious metals, the raising of stock or of falling the "tall uncut." When gold or silver veins pinched out, graze dried up or a convenient timber supply was exhausted, men moved on. Their women, good and bad must perforce trail along. Erstwhile homes, stores and hotels were left behind to decay. A city, large or small, once teeming with humans who worked, lived and loved in those buildings became a collective relic, a ghost town.

The term "ghost town" is defined with difficulty. To many it describes a village from which every vestige of living humanity has long since departed. Many of those towns described in this and previous volumes of the series present exactly such a picture of utter desertion. Others still retain a vestige or even a sizable population. Sometimes present inhabitants are true remnants of the glory days, others live there to take advantage of cheap rent. Some live in comfort in substantial homes or modern trailer units or mobile homes. In all cases, though, our "ghost towns" are ghostly in the sense that they are "shadowy semblances of their former selves," and in any case, too important in history to be excluded from any review of old camps.

Every such town inevitably had as an adjunct a burial ground. Many of these little cemeteries are populated mostly with men and women who died violently, enough to merit the popular term "Boot Hill." Included within the pale were many good, hard working citizens, men and women who represented the best in their time. Many of the stories of these people are told in our books *Boot Hill* and *Tales the Western Tombstones Tell*. Both volumes are replete with photos of the markers on their graves, weathered wooden boards or elaborately carved tombstones, some unique and all examples of a vanishing art.

At the risk of seeming to belabor an issue, we again urge the visitor to any of our old camps to "take away nothing but pictures, leave nothing but tracks." The maxim is the creed of the Mazamas, Pacific Northwest mountain climbing club of which the author is a member. Unthinking "treasure hunters" bearing modern metal detectors have been responsible for much of the hostility now frequently encountered in property owners, having irresponsibly torn down walls and ripped up floors in search of valuable relics.

About picture taking. Records of a sort may be had by simply lifting a 35 mm camera to the eye and snapping the shutter. More pleasing pictures generally merit more thought and a little more time. The author regards as essentials a good light meter, filters and consistent use of a sturdy tripod.

Good hunting!

Lambert Florin

This book is dedicated to
DAVID C. MASON, M.D.
who has done the endsheets, chapter head
drawings and maps, and in many other ways
has assisted in the preparation
of this work.

Acknowledgement

LOST MINES AND TREASURES *by Ruby El Hult*
PACIFIC GRAVEYARD *by James A. Gibbs, Jr.*
UNDER DIXIE SUN *Washington County (Utah) Historical Society*
THE BONANZA TRAIL *by Muriel Sibell Wolle*
ANYBODY'S GOLD *by Joseph Henry Jackson*
HISTORIC SPOTS IN CALIFORNIA *by Hoover and Rensch*
CALIFORNIA'S GOLDEN TREASURES *by Charles Peters*
LAND OF THE YANKEE FORK *by Esther Yarber*
HISTORICAL SILVER CITY *by Mildretta Adams*
THE MOTHER LODE, *California Division of Mines*
ROCKY TRAILS OF THE PAST *by Charles Labbe*
THE MINES BREYFOGLE MADE *by Harold Weight in Westways*
EAST OF THE CASCADES *by Phil Brogan*
OREGON FOR THE CURIOUS *by Ralph Friedman*
FEDERAL WRITERS' PROJECT GUIDE for each western state
GHOSTS OF THE ADOBE WALLS *by Nell Murbarger*
NEVADA'S TURBULENT YESTERDAYS *by Don Ashbaugh*
MONTANA PAY DIRT *by Muriel Sibell Wolle*
SHALLOW DIGGIN'S *by Jean Davis*
GUNNISON COUNTRY *by Betty Wallace*
AN EMPIRE IN SILVER *by Robert L. Brown*
COME WITH ME TO YESTERDAY and FORT STEELE
by Dave Kay and D. A. McDonald

My sincere thanks to many "Old Timers", librarians, historians and to special proof readers Gertrude and Jack Pollard.

Table of Contents

SOUTH BEND scene of misty beauty characteristic of tidal flats along mainland side of Willapa Bay. When tide is in this group of spruce-crowned trees seem to be floating unsupported. Islets are just south of South Bend whose citizens raped Oysterville's courthouse in 1892 when faster growing mainland town won position of county seat.

Washington

THE BLOOMS WERE A BEACON

*Baker's Bay (or
Chinookville, Wash.)*

A sailing ship bound for the shifting shallows of the Columbia River mouth was completely at the mercy of wind, tide and luck. Where was the channel? There were no markers, no lighthouses, no break to be seen in the low, timbered headlands obscured by fog or haze or spume from the sea pounding on the rocks and beaches. The skippers set their course by guess and St. John, put the sail gangs on point and sometimes escaped the sand spits and shoals to cross the bar into the river's yawning mouth.

The bark *Isabella* had no such luck. Out of England, bound for Fort Vancouver in the fall of 1829, she sighted the bar but lost headway in a lull, let her slack sails be caught in a sudden gale and was washed up on the sands. Capt. Thomas Ryan ordered her abandoned and all hands made shore through mountainous seas to watch the *Isabella* be pounded to kindling.

Her second mate and boatswain, Essexman James Scarborough, was one so stranded but being an experienced seaman found employment with the Hudson's Bay Co. and for ten years was master of the *Cadboro*. After his shipwreck experience he had deep compassion for skippers trying to enter the Columbia and upon taking up a homestead on the bluff above the bay where the *Isabella* came to grief, he immediately planted a grove of fruit and hawthorn trees. In succeeding years,

"THE CHINOOKS" wrote Capt. Lewis in his journal, "are low in statue, rather diminutive and ill-shapen possing thick broad, flat feet, thick ankles, crooked legs wide mouths, thick lips, nose moderately large fleshy, wide at the extremity with large nostrils, black eyes and coarse hair, their eyes are sometimes of a dark yellowish brown the puple black. The most remarkable trait in their physiognomy is the peculiar flatness and width of forehead which is artificially obtained by compressing the head between two boards while in a state of infancy and from which it never afterwards perfectly recovers" . . . (Photo Smithsonian Institution).

OLD PRINT of British ship **Tonquin**, anchored in harbor then called Haley's Bay, officially Baker's Bay, in 1811. John Jacob Astor sent out two parties, one overland led by Wilson Price Hunt, one by sea captained by crusty Jonathan Thorn. Latter was one of several to select site of what would be Astoria. **Tonquin** sailed from here to Clayoquot Sound, Vancouver Island, where it met disaster through attacks by Indians and explosion (Photo Smithsonian Institution).

MARKER AT BAKER'S BAY (Chinookville). Capt. Clark noted in his journal. "The tide meeting of me and the emence swells from the Main Ocian raised to such a hite that I concluded to form a camp on the highest spot I could find . . . in the upper part of Haley's Bay . . . This Chinook Nation is about 400 Souls inhabited the country on Small rivers that run into the bay directly below us . . . I directed all the men who wished to see more of the main Ocian to prepare themselves to set out with me early on tomorrow morning. The principal Chief of the Chinooks came to see us this evening." The "Chief" would have been one-eyed Concomly (see Boot Hill).

when the trees were in full bloom, the sheet of white blossoms on Scarborough Head was conspicuous for many miles on the lower river, a beacon seen even out at sea.

At the base of the Head near the beach was a Chinook Indian village of perhaps 300 to 400 natives, the community existing many years before advent of the white man. Among the first of these were men named Svipton, "One-Eyed" Skelly and Haley, an adjacent inlet first called after him, Haley's Bay.

When Capt. Bruno Heceta sailed up the Columbia about the time of our American revolution he indicated the bay as "Bahia de la Ascuncion". Thirteen years later Capt. John Meares named it "Deception Bay". Lewis and Clark had other ideas and it became "Rogue's Harbor". Later Capt. Baker of the brig *Jenny* anchored there and no doubt unaware that the water was topheavy with names, bestowed yet another on it—his own. And Baker's Bay it has remained.

By the custom of most white men alone in Indian country, Capt. Scarborough in 1843 married a Chinook woman, Ann Elizabeth, a member of the tribe in the village on the site of Chinookville, across the river from Fort Astoria. At one time the tribe was headed by famous one-eyed Chief Concomly (see *Boot Hill*).

The young couple took up a donation land claim of 640 acres which included part of Concomly's domain as well as Scarborough Head or Hill. Besides his fruit trees and shrubs the captain raised stock animals picked up on his voyages. He built a house shared with his Indian wife, contrary to custom, and to them were born four sons, only two surviving.

During these years Capt. Scarborough had his hand in many business ventures such as shipping fish to England and serving as river pilot. A mystery begins with the story of his having been paid for these efforts over the years in gold ingots amounting to $60,000, and that he buried the fortune somewhere on the hill. In February of 1855 the captain died suddenly without divulging the location of the ingots. James Burney of Cathlamet took the two boys in, one of them, Ned, living to be 80, dying at Cathlamet about 1925.

In 1864 the government bought the Scarborough estate as being a strategic location for defense of the Columbia. About 1894 Fort Columbia was built on the site, becoming a state park after the end of World War II.

Presumably the treasure is still somewhere about, apparently not discovered in the building of the fort or highway through the park. There remains a large area still undisturbed, too large for a search without a clue. Ruby El Hult, author of *Lost Mines and Treasures*, estimates the present value of the gold ingots to be about $120,000.

TIDEFLAT TABLEAU

Nahcotta, Wash.

"Folks, you are now in Oysterland, U.S.A."

"I don't care about oysters. I can't eat the slithery things."

"Well, I'm sorry, lady. If I was anything more than the conductor of this train I'd get you some crepes suzette."

"When does this train get to Nahcotta? It's over an hour late and my sister will be frozen to death waiting for it."

"Oh I don't know. She's probably keeping warm and happy eating oysters. They're fine for the blood."

Some such spirited conversation might have taken place on the Ilwaco and Shoalwater Bay Railroad or was it the Ilwaco Railway and Navigation Co. or maybe this week the Oregon and Washington Railway and Navigation Co.? Sometimes the "noon" train would come puff-puffing into the tiny station at Nahcotta on time but more often it would arrive at 11 or perhaps 1. While travelers got nervous, residents understood that schedules depended upon the ocean tides at the mouth of the Columbia River since the main reason for the existence of the narrow-gauge line was its connection with the ferry from Astoria, Oregon.

The Chinooks were the original settlers at Nahcotta, their villages once dotting the entire North Peninsula. An ample food supply was guaranteed them by the millions of oysters growing wild on the flats of the harbor. Innumerable food middens still evident today show oyster shells their main content. No primitive tools are found with them as oysters require only to be picked up at low tide and pried open.

The abundance of bivalves and fish attracted whites too, the first to arrive at Nahcotta as a resident being J. A. Morehead in 1890. He was shortly joined by James R. Morrison and eight other men, some with families to form a fair-sized village. With later settlers came a store, Morehead building one to contain the post office, Morrison being the first to handle the mail. There was unanimous agreement in naming the town for old Chief Nahcotta who was still camping on the outskirts. While lacking the power of Chief Concomly at nearby Chinookville, Nahcotta displayed the same friendly attitude toward the whites.

In 1899 the town became the terminus of the short line railroad running on narrow-gauge tracks which over the years had so many names the Nahcotta station master A. P. Osborne sometimes forgot just who he was working for. By 1908 the train was running on a regular schedule and continued to until 1930. Until recently traces of trackage were visible in places along the line.

Once boasting a weekly newspaper edited by John Phillips, Nahcotta is today a resort settlement with two small industries—a sweater knitting "factory" and one punching and stringing oyster shells for nurturing baby shellfish.

OLD OYSTER BARGE, one of once large fleet at Nahcotta beached away from water except during flood tides. Flat-decked vessel took large empty baskets to anchorage over oyster beds. Baskets were filled at low tide and reloaded on barges which floated at high tide and were towed to oyster plants. In background is Willapa Bay, early termed Shoalwater Bay. In middle distance are rotting pilings, all that remain of large railroad terminal dock. Body of water, considered to be prehistoric channel of Columbia River, offered exact condition of alternating fresh and salt water demanded by oyster. While tide is out bay is freshened by flow from many rivers. Returning tides obstruct streams temporarily providing high salinity. Sometimes strong offshore winds and high tides force in oversupply of salty water, preventing breeding, even killing some stock.

OLD POSTCARD shows Nahcotta when narrow-gauge railroad had terminus here. Hotel at end of rails was important then, has vanished now. Water supply was pumped by windmill and stored in tank left.

THE TOWN THAT OYSTERS BUILT

Oysterville, Wash.

The pilot of the river steamer looked with disdain at all the industry displayed in harvesting the flat, curly-edged shells in the low tide mud. "It's sure a good thing I don't like oysters," he said, "or I'd eat 'em and I hate the damn things!"

There are deeply etched opinions about the succulence of oysters but the early workers on the Pacific Ocean beach cared little about that. They had a tide flat gold mine in millions of the bivalves lying there defenseless in the oozy muck just waiting to be picked, shipped to market and opened before eyes bulging in anticipation. "Too good for Indians," they said.

When the white man first came to Willapa (then called Shoalwater) Bay he found its south arm one vast field of oyster beds. The native marine bivalves were the small, delicately flavored *ostrea lurida*. For them and the later introduced Pacific oysters, the bay offered perfect conditions for reproduction and growth. The oyster requires an almost exactly formulated mixture of fresh and salt water and the saline content must vary at specific intervals. Willapa Bay, like very few harbors on the Washington coast, offers the right mixture, an inflow of fresh water supplied by the Naselle and other rivers while the tide is at full or receding, supplying an alternating flood of salt water from the ocean. Native Chinook tribes had long made the shellfish a major item of food but this local consumption had hardly dented the supply.

The first white to see commercial possibilities here was very likely young Virginia-born Charles Russell. For several decades the United States had been on an oyster binge, consuming huge quantities in all forms, appetite whetted by rumor that oysters would enlarge or resuscitate the libido. Russell was aware that during the time the non-ambulatory oyster was exposed by outgoing tides it closed its valves tightly, excluding desiccating air. He also knew this normally short hibernation period could be extended.

The only entrance to Willapa Bay was at the north end, some 30 miles north of the Columbia River from which Russell would ship his oysters to San Francisco. In prehistoric times the Columbia had at least partially emptied its waters into the now separated northern estuary, the old channel now low and watery or marshy in spots. This route was used by Indians for centuries as a portage connection from the Columbia. In the summer of 1851, with a partner, Russell took a canoe over this route to the bay and at low tide walked over the flats, easily collecting a load of oysters which he took back to Astoria. The cargo reached San Francisco in good condition and was sold at a good price. When gourmets there clamored for more they expanded the life purpose of *ostrea lurida*.

Heartened by visions of success Russell put into action ambitious plans to improve the southern access route to the source of supply. Meanwhile he learned that a Capt. Fielstad had run a schooner direct from San Francisco to Willapa Bay, entering

OLD POSTCARD version of Oysterville's famed courthouse, forcibly entered by rival residents of South Bend across bay to remove county records.

PACIFIC HOUSE, Oysterville's largest hostelry of which no trace remains. Likely not all people in old photo were patrons though hotel did big business while town flourished.

LINES OF PILING, weathered to silvery gray, indicate location of wharf where sailing ships loaded live oysters for San Francisco markets. Here also were tied barges that placed empty picking baskets, later retrieving filled ones at next high tide. Long unused baskets now rust away, half-filled with sand, oyster shells. Willapa Bay is in background.

by the easy but farther north entrance south of Cape Shoalwater. Hard on his stern were the schooners *Sea Serpent* and *Robert Bruce*, other ships following. One was delayed by a storm when sailing south, the cargo spoiling, and one burned to the water's edge by a mutinous cook. The oyster rush was on.

In 1854 R. H. Espy of Wisconsin arrived at the bay to locate and supply logs for pilings. A man of strong religious principles he invited I. A. Clark, of similar background and who had some money, to become his partner. While scouring the shores of the bay they became enthused with the possibilities of commercially canning the abundantly available oysters. Abandoning the piling venture Espy and Clark built a log house on the spot where the town of Oysterville would develop, the location between sea and bay near the northern tip of the peninsula.

Then came the brothers John and Thomas Crellin to share in the oyster profits, John establishing a mercantile store. With rapid growth the little town was demanding mail service and got it in 1865, the post office set up in a corner of Crellin's store. Mail had to be carried over devious Indian trails from Chinookville.

After a few years of such primitive service Lewis Loomis, who was to become a big man in Oysterville's history, secured the mail contract. In 1875 he and his partners built the 110-foot, screw-drive *General Canby* at Willapa at the northern end of the bay, the vessel undoubtedly named for the ill-fated army officer who died at the hands of Captain Jack in the still fresh Modoc War (see *Tales the Western Tombstones Tell*). As soon as launched, the ship was put into service carrying mail and passengers from Astoria, Oregon, to Ilwaco, Washington, where they were dumped on the beach.

13

OLD ANCHOR AND BUOY are few of marine items in machine repair shops of near-defunct Columbia River Smokery.

If time and tide were right, a stagecoach that was humanely called "clumsy" picked them up.

Powered by eight broncos the wooden vehicle was closed at the ends, passengers admitted from one side. There were seats inside for five but what was that when twenty people climbed in? Two would cling to the mail-loaded boot at the rear, others perched on top and when all were aboard the coach bumped and swayed onto the wet sand recently vacated by the Pacific, then headed north.

In recent years the North Jetty at the mouth of the Columbia River has diverted river-born sands northward, building up a beach far-famed for length and width. In the 1870s the beach was narrower and the stagecoach was sometimes forced to take to the dunes, humping itself over the sandy hillocks and small pieces of driftwood. The region has a heavy annual rainfall and when frequent ocean storms lashed the coast those unlucky passengers on top must have deeply regretted embarking for Oysterville.

The village had become seat of Pacific County some time before the first schoolhouse was erected, lumber for which was California redwood shipped

north on a schooner that returned with canned and smoked oysters. The arrival at Oysterville of the ship was celebrated by a general holiday. When all sobered up the entire town joined with the hired carpenters in putting up the little schoolhouse and painting it bright red. The first teacher was James Pell.

Ten years later, with growing pains subsiding, residents began to think of social festivities, something more dramatic than box lunch suppers and community dances. With all that water around why not stage a yacht race? After several small but successful annual events, the town went all out in 1876 with a well advertised regatta that attracted such famous racers as the sloop *Artemisia* owned by wealthy Ed Loomis. The affair attracted the entire population of the coastal area, and a large contingent of "city folk" arrived from Portland on the specially-chartered steamer *Gussie Telfair.*

Shortly after Oysterville became a village much of Washington was being harassed by rampaging Indians, the troubles threatening to explode into a full scale war. Towns and settlements along the west coast were thrown into panic, most of them erecting blockhouses. Oysterville did so, hastily building a log fort near the water. While the structure still lacked a roof, townsfolk realized their placid, friendly Chinook neighbors were laughing at their efforts and sheepish carpenters left the project unfinished.

In the expanding community by the bay the main street was called "Front," built largely on rocks brought in as ship ballast and piled along the edge of the harbor to be close to canneries and vessels. The village so near the water was vulnerable to extremes of high tides which all too often demolished whole buildings when high winds combined with high water. One storm took away the roofless fort.

Oysterville was the seat of Pacific County very early but for years no actual courthouse was built. In 1860 a man named Dupenny was accused of murdering the Indian wife of a neighbor, William McGunnegill. Constable Espy was forced to board the suspect in his home temporarily before transferring him to the more secure Army barracks jail at Fort Vancouver. Even so nothing was done about the situation until 1869. Then the county erected a substantial two-story structure set on a foundation of squared logs.

During the decade of 1880-1890 Oysterville enjoyed its greatest days of glory. The first really adequate wharf was extended into deep water in

'84, another built in '88. A newspaper, first in the county, was established in 1887. Called the *Pacific Journal*, it was edited by "Alf" Bowen.

The 1890s were not "gay" for the oyster center of North Peninsula. The shellfish were found elsewhere on Willapa Bay and rival town South Bend had grown up on the shore opposite. The upstart had the unfair advantage of being on the mainland at a strategic point in the stagecoach system, and close to forests, it soon had a large lumbering industry.

In the fall elections of 1892 South Bend was declared the new seat of Pacific County and all records were ordered delivered there. Oysterville ignored the summons, the town's hardy, brine-soaked citizenry refusing to give up the honor of county seat, claiming the South Bend electorate had illegally included residents of all surrounding communities. Authorities were successful in obtaining an injunction but before this could be put into effect, ambitious promoters of the rival town forced the issue.

On February 5, 1893, a cold day dawning over a snowy scene unusual for the peninsula, two steamboats docked at Oysterville. Eighty-five men swarmed off and converged on the courthouse. Auditor Phil D. Barney was the first to assess the invasion and when South Bend leader John Hudson kicked in the courthouse door, the enraged Barney broke off a chair leg and valiantly attempted to defend the records by cracking several enemy skulls. A witness to the fracas was 6-year-old C. J. Espy who says, "I hid behind the door and was scared to death but I saw the action." Overpowered, Barney was forced to watch the removal of all paper except that in his vault, the key to which he steadfastly refused to give up. Later, however, other Oysterville authorities persuaded him that further resistance would be futile.

Although later investigation proved the South Bend election was highly irregular, counting ballots of transient loggers and other non-registered voters, the situation was by now irreversible. Staggered by the blow Oysterville mourned the loss of the courthouse for two years then decided to put the

LITTLE BAPTIST CHURCH was built in 1870s by Oysterville's founder, R. H. Espy, photo made some years ago. When author returned to Oysterville in 1967 to make more recent one, he found church being restored. Repairs are being made by son C. J. Espy who reported that services were held until "community interest dwindled to a point that continuance of regular services seem inappropriate. Sunday School was maintained until about 1942. Since then occasional funerals and weddings have been held there. There seems to be no immediate or early rejuvenation of service activities, only a hope by the writer and his family who, for sentimental reasons are giving some attention to the upkeep of the physical edifice."

INTERIOR of Baptist Church in Oysterville. No one, including builder's son C. J. Espy can explain why pews are divided in center. He does report structure never had electricity except temporarily in recent years when church was lit for wedding by extension cables powering borrowed light fixtures. Original light came from two large chandeliers with circles of lamps, suspended from ceiling on ropes, lowered for filling with kerosene and wick-trimming. After years of faithful service one crashed down on pews. Though accident happened in midweek, potential danger to worshippers caused removal of chandeliers and use of small wall lamps seen here. When founder-builder R. H. Espy died his casket was squeezed into tiny sanctuary leaving little space for passage.

OLD COLUMBIA RIVER SMOKERY is now mostly idle, small crew operating part of equipment in winter, smoking and canning limited catch.

empty building to practical use. In 1895 a brash sign announced it was the new "Peninsula College." Courses scheduled studies in grade and high school subjects, the initial enthusiasm bringing in forty students. Tuition was $30 for nine months. A faculty of six was hired and the institution opened. At the end of the first year the student body dwindled to half, the second showed fewer. The college closed and the building suffered ignominy as a cow barn, in recent years collapsing through heavy weather and neglect.

Little is now left to indicate the existence of a town large enough to support several hotels, saloons, stores. In addition to being remotely situated, Oysterville's prosperity was based on a single industry. When the once ample supply of oysters vanished, so did the economy.

The few present residents of the town are mostly descendants of pioneers, notably C. J. Espy. He recalls that during the period of prosperity every out-of-town visitor was sooner or later regaled with a bit of doggerel:

> Said one oyster to another
> In tones of pure delight,
> "I will meet you in the kitchen
> And we'll both get stewed tonight."

BEAUTIFUL HOUSE might be termed Victorian, displaying uniquely elaborate barge boards. Built in 1869 as home of pioneer Tom Crellins, it became home of Harry Espy, elder son of founder, who grew up here and was father of Dr. R. H. Espy, Gen. Sec. of Nat. Council of Churches, N.Y.C. Next door is 1871 house built by town's founder and birthplace of C. J. Espy who, now in his 80s, sleeps in room of nativity.

McCORMICK—Charles R. McCormick Lumber Co. mills turned out quantities of columns, used product for porch of company offices. Long after demise of operations, Lewis County bought building for use as tubercular hospital. Rock Creek Sanitarium served while "open air" method of treatment prevailed.

OLD FRAME HOUSE was once residence of McCormick Mill official, later served as quarters for employees of tuberculosis sanitarium. Decaying structure still displays elegant architectural touches in fanfanlight, columned portico.

WEATHERED WALLS of old garage at junction of graveled road outside Dryad. Town given poetical name of forest nymph in 1901 by unknown representative of Leudinghaus Lumber Co. surveying timber lands just east of Rainbow Falls on Chehalis River. His firm moved in but in 1905 all properties were lost in total fire. Entire plant was rebuilt but today all this is gone as are most houses where loggers and lumbermen lived. Fertile "beaver lands" in bottoms are still cultivated to some extent, hillsides mostly barren clay since stripped of forest cover.

PE ELL, name being Indian pronunciation of French "Pierre," settler who took advantage of grassy patches in heavy timber along Chehalis River for grazing his horses. Later whites, like Amor Mauerman who platted town, retained name. Pioneers in 1890 staved off starvation, cold, by killing deer, other wild game for food, pelts. Wild life remained abundant many years. **The Coast,** published in Seattle, said in 1902, "D. V. Thrash, one of the earliest settlers...killed over 400 bear and deer since his coming to this place. On Sept. 7 of this year a cougar 7 feet 2 inches long was killed two miles from town." Always dependent upon logs, lumber for cash income, Pe Ell still leans on operations of Weyerhaeuser Co.

FLAG IN THE TALL TIMBER

Claquato, Wash.

All that scary talk! Why these northern Indians in Washington Territory were so friendly they were going to show him how to put up a temporary camp in the forest against the wet winter weather and even help him and his boys build it. The plains Indians were warlike and troublesome but these fellows pointed out a big fir tree where he could put up the camp and by Jupiter, he'd call it the "Pioneer Tree"!

So did the first family start life on the hill called Claquato, a high place, by the Indians on the south side of the Chehalis River. They hacked out a crude road to a shallow place in the river where they could ford it and haul in the household goods brought up from Portland.

This was the Lewis Hawkins Davis family from back east. He was born in Windsor County, Vermont, and went west to Fort Wayne, Indiana, becoming a partner in a sawmill venture. He married Susan A. Clinger and fathered five sons and two daughters. In 1852 it seemed the whole country was headed westward for the fertile Willamette Valley in Oregon. On fire with the idea of carving out a new home in a new country, Davis and family joined a wagon train out of Independence, Missouri, and arrived in the village of Portland near the end of the same year. Some twenty-two months of casting around the area convinced Davis it was already too crowded, some farms being within a mile or two of each other.

Hearing much talk of good farm lands available farther north, he and family set out again, this time on a boat going down the Willamette to the Columbia River. At its junction with another tributary, the Cowlitz, the party went upstream to Cowlitz Landing, then a pioneer settlement. The surrounding country looked good to Davis but he selected an area centered by a rise of land and took out a donation land claim.

By 1855 the Indians had turned bitter, realizing that unless the increasing white tide was stemmed, they were doomed. Skirmishes with settlers all over western Washington caused the government to authorize the building of stockades and block-houses as protective measures. At Claquato Davis got the local contract, providing manpower and logs. The structure was built on the brow of the hill just west of the town center, the always hungry workers fed by Mrs. Davis from a kitchen set up on the site. When the building was finished all families moved in but after many quarrels natural to strangers in cramped quarters, they returned to their homes.

The first settlers built cabins of logs cut from the smaller trees. The hill was not solidly forested and opening it up increased pasture area. In 1857 Davis built a whipsaw sawmill at the bottom of the hill where little Mill Creek flows into the Chehalis. A pool was enlarged to hold logs skidded in by ox team. A dedicated Methodist, Davis used his first produced lumber to build a church.

Fortunately for the community a good craftsman was available, one who easily doubled as architect— John Duff Clinger, brother of Mrs. Davis. He planned the structure in entirety and personally

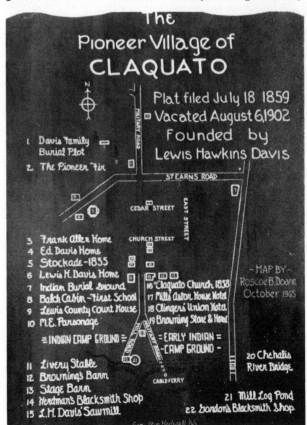

"BILLBOARD" near Claquato Church gives quick run-down on one of most historic towns in state.

SUNDAY SCHOOL, occasional services, were held in old building until mid-'30s when slow destruction by vandals began, doors then padlocked, windows boarded up. Restoration was begun in early '50s by Chehalis Post No. 22, American Legion and county officials. No structural changes were necessary, all original materials left in place with few exceptions. New wallpaper utilized old pattern as used in churches a century ago. Renovated church was rededicated Aug. 16, 1953.

made door and window casings. He built the unusual steeple, framing it with mortise and tenon work of finest quality. Even the lookouts supporting the roof projection on the gables were mortised and wedged into the end rafters. As the oldest building still standing in the State of Washington the unique church is a monument to John Clinger.

The crude little mill was pushed to its limit, its lumber snapped up for more construction. In a short time the hill was crowned by two hotels, blacksmith shop, carpenter and cabinet shops, livery stable and church parsonage which with several houses constituted Claquato, the largest village between Monticello and Olympia.

Davis was astute in realizing the growing town

must have more systematic planning and hired Henry H. Stearns, surveyor and one of the original immigrants, to legally lay out the site. The resulting plat was filed with the county clerk on July 18, 1859. It shows the location of the church already built and four lots deeded to the county by Davis on which he intended to build a two-story courthouse and deed that to the county too.

By the next year when construction started an extra set of gears had been added to the shaft in the mill so water power could be used for grinding wheat and corn. In the spring with ample stream flow both operations could be handled simultaneously. The trouble was, most grist was made shortly after late summer harvest when water was low. Some farmers were forced to cool their heels while enough lumber was cut to keep courthouse builders on the job and on occasion they were forced to wait until grain growers were satisfied. In spite of these and other delays the structure received the finishing touches early in 1862.

The Civil War was raging now and while it hardly whispered into the northwest corner the Claquato women were resolved to be patriotic and make a flag that would be a credit to the new courthouse. John H. Browning, son-in-law of Davis and owner of the general store, was in San Francisco buying supplies when he received a letter from his wife telling him to bring home materials for a flag 18 by 36 feet. Although convinced the size given was in error he returned in mid-April with $90 worth of cloth and thread. In his home the women hand stitched thousands of feet of seams to complete the giant emblem. A crew of men scoured the forest to find a big tree of proper proportions. Trimmed, peeled and brought home, it was placed in a 20-foot hole, then standing 120 feet tall.

And then for the dedication of the courthouse. The war demanded immense quantities of medical materials called "sanitary supplies." An inspired suggestion was approved—to call the planned affair the "Sanitation Ball," all proceeds to go to the war effort. The big day came on the Fourth of July, 1862. At 10 a.m. minister John Harwood opened the ceremony with prayer. Then thirteen men, one for each of the original colonies, fired four volleys and the flag was slowly raised to the top of the pole while the townspeople sang a hymn. After a picnic by the river, Mills Brothers orchestra arrived from Olympia and the dance was begun, to end in a blaze of "Old Glory." Tickets sold at $5 each and after all expenses, such as $50 in gold for the band, there remained a grand total of $250 for the sanitation fund. The flag was flown daily for the remainder of the war but on one sad day, October 22, 1864, it was lowered to half-mast for Lewis H. Davis.

The town's founder had suffered a bad fall in his mill and he lingered in agony for several weeks without recovering. The funeral was held in the little church he built, his body borne past the courthouse and on up the hill to the small cemetery and laid to rest not far from the Pioneer Fir.

With the patriarch's death some changes came to Claquato. Most of his activities were taken over by his grown sons but the Davis stage line, initiated by Henry Winsor and Rice Tilly of Olympia in 1861 and which ran from Monticello to Olympia with Claquato as an overnight stop,

was sold to a Mr. Coggins who was killed by Indians later. In 1865 the big flag was again lowered in mourning for Abraham Lincoln.

The Indian scare of the middle '50s that brought tragedy and death to other Washington communities never directly affected Claquato and the building of the fort was entirely futile. Local Indians became friendly and cooperative as in the founding days, small groups camping nearby for many years. Probably the best remembered native was "Queen Susan," wife of a powerful chief in the area. She was still young and attractive when he died and could have married a brave of high rank, instead falling in love with a slave. When she married him outraged members of the tribe rejected her but, as royalty, permitted her to remain, with the same lowly status as her mate. When he died the middle-aged and fat widow lived among the whites at Claquato. Dressed in brilliant cast-off clothing she went from house to house doing any kind of cleaning or laundering chores for a living. Her cheerful nature was a bright light in the community.

Susan died in 1868 and the citizens gave her a funeral as imposing as one the tribe would have given her as queen. Most townspeople attended and schools were closed for the day. Even the passengers of two stages which stopped for a change of horses witnessed the rites. All Indians living within several miles also came, having forgotten their queen's descent from grace. Susan's body was taken to the foot of the hill and placed in the Indian burial ground. No marker remains on her grave or that of any other native.

The town on the old Military Road, then the main traveled artery between the Columbia River and Olympia, was shrugged aside when rails were laid in 1874. The line now ran through Saundersville, where Davis camped when locating a homesite. With subsequent growth that town became Chehalis and eventually took the county seat from Claquato, which was officially vacated in county records of August 6, 1902.

HISTORIC PIONEER FIR, identified by bronze plaque fastened to trunk. Gigantic specimen sheltered immigrants 116 years ago, was huge then. This form of branching rare in fir. Location is near center of Claquato cemetery.

OLD KING COAL IS DEAD

Who ever heard of a coal rush? Yet Roslyn had several—the sudden influx of miners in 1886, rushes in and out of town when it was beset by fires, strikes, explosions and competition from nearby Ronald. There was "never a dull moment" in this coal center of the pine woods.

The railroad set off the first blast. The Northern Pacific needed a west coast source of good coal and this area was only four miles north of its main line. The first coal was packed out of outcroppings by horses in 1883 and three years later the Northern Pacific Railroad sent a corps of experts in to probe the protruding black ledges along Smith Creek east of Stampede Pass. What they found was coal of a quality and quantity that encouraged a survey for a branch line up the creek bed from Cle Elum. By act of Congress the company already owned every other section of land in the region which included this coal and within weeks more than a hundred men were working at the outcropping veins. Some brought their families and the result was an almost instant town.

Logan M. Bullitt platted it and with a romantic gesture named it Roslyn after a sweetheart in a Delaware town of that name. Dedication papers were filed in Minnesota September 22, 1886, with local legalities for Kittitas County taken care of six days later. Most streets were laid out sixty feet wide with Pennsylvania eighty. By December 13, it was evident an addition would be needed and this was platted at the northeast corner of the original townsite. Almost immediately still another became necessary to accommodate all the new arrivals.

The first iron horse brought a wave of them, mostly miners from Italy, followed by others from Austria and Slavic countries and Negroes in quantity. That first winter saw some four hundred men congregated in camp.

Company officials were well aware that a percentage of them would be rascals, male and

SPIRALED STRIPS OF STEEL are long undisturbed shavings from machine shops at lower edge of Roslyn.

female, and since it was a company town they were determined to keep it as peaceful as human nature would allow. Gambling dens were strictly prohibited and officially absent for many years but that did not prevent some clandestine poker games and cock-fights.

To curb excess drinking the company set up its own saloon, which with a general store were the first business structures in town. One individual lot buyer erected a building across the street from the company enterprise, getting little trade until the word "Saloon" was painted on its false front. Then the owner got the Sunday punch and a padlock on the door. He was instructed to read the fine print in his deed, a clause strictly forbidding manufacture or sale of intoxicating liquors.

Inevitably another saloon went up, but on private land just outside the town limits in the "tall uncut." Two more followed it and then another, so labeled but actually a spot where a lonely coal miner could find a warm embrace for a price.

Rumor had it several men not reporting for work had been rolled and dragged into the heavy forest. All this forced the town bosses to allow legitimate saloons within town limits where they could be regulated.

Other pioneer buildings were the hotel (corporation owned) that housed a hundred men, boarding house and two livery stables. All were built of lumber cut in the company owned sawmill from company owned timber.

The first half of 1888 saw a briskly flourishing Roslyn with some 1200 population. On June 22, about four o'clock in the afternoon smoke was seen coming from a building between First and Second. The alarm was sounded, a futile gesture with so little fire protection available, for within two hours all buildings were in ruins. Loss was about $100,000 and that meant loss for most property owners felt the 10% insurance premium was exhorbitant.

In a few months Roslyn was on its way to recovery, many new buildings springing up from

NO. 3 MINE, altho part of Roslyn complex, warranted separate town of Ronald for convenience, businesses, rooming houses, saloons. Although later mines like No. 9, 10, were fairly good producers, none ever surpassed production, importance of old No. 3.

PARTLY OCCUPIED, partly boarded up house is typical of many old homes in Roslyn, once flourishing coal camp, deterioration now well under way.

the ashes and an era of prosperity prevailed. Then in August came the first of several labor uprisings. An organization called the Knights of Labor was organizing unions all over the country and in July of 1888 almost all Roslyn miners were made "brothers," the few dissenters made miserable. The town was fertile ground in which to plant and cultivate seeds of strike against the Northern Pacific mine owners. Wages were small, working hours stretched to ten, miners working under constant threat of explosions and collapsing tunnels.

The ensuing strike was long and bloody incidents frequent. Most workers had little or no backlog on which to subsist and some had to leave town. Mine officials imported crews of Negroes as "scabs," many remaining after the settlement to account for much of Roslyn's population to its very end. Among scanty details of the strike is the item that officials called for martial law but the settlement was reached before soldiers were sent in.

By December of 1890 all miners were working full time, the monthly payroll $84,000. Then when the owners lost the Union Pacific contract the payroll shrank to $63,000 and lean days came until new contracts were secured. Then the famous producer, Mine No. 3, one mile away, was opened and all was rosy again, the town of Ronald growing up around the new mine, named after Alexander Ronald, a mine superintendent.

In the midst of happy prosperity came the disastrous explosion of May 9, 1892. A noontime underground blast took the lives of forty-five men. A relief committee was quickly organized and gathered $7,000 from outside communities, $2,000 from Roslyn citizens, the fund aided by supplies collected by Knights of Pythias and other organizations. 36% of it went to widows, the remainder to the fatherless children.

That same year on September 24, bandits got away with a small fortune from the town's bank, Ben E. Snipes Co., and more money was spent in a futile attempt to solve the crime. The bank may have been thinly financed for on June 9 of the next year its doors were closed in the face of a clamoring mob of depositors who lost $100,000. The blow was a crippling tragedy as the sum represented all savings in the community. Some depositors eventually received certificates of indebtedness, "good for framing," as one man said. The next year saw a strike in May over wages which lasted several months, greatly depressing business and working hardships.

Yet things brightened up at the end of 1896. One reason seems to be the progressive ideas of B. F. Bush who came to Roslyn as manager of the coal company's operations that year. He put into practice a more liberal policy which increased the number of working days to six per week which was still not enough to supply the coal in demand. For the next seven years the town enjoyed the full dinner pail, fat pocketbook and comfortable home.

OLD MINE CAR stands idle with others in lots once occupied by business buildings, long made empty by series of destructive fires.

POWER HOUSE, generating steam, part of complex of once busy warehouses, machine shops etc., adjacent to old railroad yards.

A murder shocked the town on the morning of Friday, March 20, 1896. The brutally bludgeoned body of the well-liked company doctor, J. H. Lyon, was found a few feet from his own doorstep. The apparent weapon was a table leg lying a few feet away, covered with blood and hair, pocketbook and jewelry untouched on his body. The last person to see Dr. Lyon was his long-time friend, merchant Samuel Isaacs. Enraged townspeople collected $400 as reward for the murderer's arrest and conviction to which was added $500 by the state governor, $300 by Kittitas County and $300 by the city of Roslyn.

Suspicion eventually fell on two brothers known to have made threats against the doctor, accusing him of what amounted to malpractice in treating a third brother. The evidence was slim and they were released after a preliminary hearing, the record stating, "Mystery still enshrouds one of the blackest crimes ever committed in the history of the State of Washington."

In the same period the town was struck down by an epidemic of diphtheria. After several deaths all schools were closed, all public gatherings banned. On the heels of this came another. Smallpox spread rapidly, blame placed on admitted poor sanitary conditions in the town. When this scare subsided, Roslyn again went forward.

In 1904 the population was some 4,000 made up mainly of Slavs, Negroes, Italians and Germans. By this time the mines were privately owned, 1898 legislation denying railroads the right to operate mines of any kind. In 1909 another mine explosion took ten lives. By 1930 the population was down to 2,289, the decline continuing steadily. Today the town, not entirely dead, displays many examples of Victorian elegance in its surviving buildings, some of them still occupied.

POWDER HOUSE building solidly built of stone and iron-shuttered, still stands at Ronald, "suburb" of Roslyn. It held large supplies of blasting powder for coal mines but stored well away as accidental explosion might collapse mine shoring.

UNION, not actually a ghost, is community full of history but depleted in population. Located in extreme southeast corner of Grand Ronde Valley air currents from Pyle's Canyon drain away some of severest frosts. Conrad Miller, who first settled here about 1860, noted comparatively mild winters, left his cabin in 1862 to get fruit trees and supplies. Returning home he found his claim occupied by Fred Nordlund and others but reestablished it and started one of first nurseries in area. Almost immediately after other settlers arrived Union became center of cross roads from mines to mountains. Civil War caused intense feelings among residents majority of whom had northern sympathies and named town. First flag was made by local women from odds and ends of red, white and blue cloth, unfurled at 4th of July celebration in 1863. Classic example of false-front architecture shown here still stands on main street, relic of Union's earliest days. Many other elaborate examples of later Victorian style are found in fine old houses on back streets.

Oregon

GOLD — AND A GENIUS

Canyon City, Oregon

While its diggings yielded many millions in gold, Canyon City's history is colored more vividly by the character of one of its citizens. This was the bearded poet Cincinnatus Heine Miller, more familiarly known as Joaquin Miller who doubled as squaw man, prospector, printer's devil, supply packer and who as county judge claimed he "dispensed justice in Canyon City with a six-shooter in each hand."

In the early 1860s an unknown number of men combed the canyons and gulches of eastern Oregon, most of them on the trail of the mysterious Blue Bucket Mine. Although that location was never positively identified many other rich diggings were located. No one can say how much gold may have been or still is in the Blue Bucket but certainly Canyon Creek gave up a whopping $8 million in dust and nuggets. Among many stories of the original discovery in 1862 is the one that has the unlikely elements so often founded on fact. One of these is that in the first party camping on Whiskey Flat, a scant half mile north of where the town would grow, was one Billy Aldred who strayed from the others to make his own explorations. Spotting a location he liked across a creek, he waded over and found the gravel promising. Being without a pan or container for samples he stripped off his long underwear and by knotting the ankles and wrists, made four long bags which he filled

HERE LIVED JOAQUIN MILLER, described as "a bit of a charlatan . . . a restless, spectacular character, capable of writing an occasional poem with a vigorous lilt." Arriving here with wife Minnie and baby in 1864, controversial poet brought first fruit trees, ornamental shrubs to raw mining camp on pack animals. Double white lilacs shown left and right could be survivors of original shrubs.

Chair, hand cut from single section of log is on porch of Joaquin Miller cabin at Canyon City. Long extended periods of sitting in it would seem to invite case of curvature of spine.

with gold laden sand. Three days later a saloon was erected on the spot and other structures followed it. Canyon City was on its way. At the peak of the rush some 10,000 people of every description thronged the narrow main street called Whiskey Gulch.

Breaking through the crowds were numerous trains of oxen, mules and horses bringing in supplies from The Dalles by way of the old Military Road, animals and wagons having crossed swollen rivers, stretches of desert sand and rocky mountain defiles. Indians lurked at several points, the danger increasing as they learned the value of gold coming back with the teams.

With the influx of packers, miners and traders came the inevitable gamblers and prostitutes. One of the former was a notorious card sharp known as Black Dan because of his swarthy complexion. The story told about him is the one credited to some gambler in almost every mountain camp, yet it could have happened to him. Caught by a bullet, Black Dan could see his end approaching but requested his saloon buddies to "lay him out" as already dead, and bring in some of the girls. The going away party got rolling with a toast to the near-departed when it was discovered he had

been so inconsiderate as to spoil everything by not waiting for the glasses to be drained.

Independence Day celebrations in early mining camps were rated next to Christmas in importance and featured sack races, football games and volunteer fire department drills. In 1863 Canyon City staged a Fourth of July affair that got somewhat out of hand. With the Civil War raging there was some violence between miners, prospectors and hangers-on who had Confederate or Union sympathies and on this occasion with saloons filled quarrels sprang up quickly. Supporters of the South, largely from California, and Union men from Oregon, Washington and Idaho, let their feelings and tempers grow hotter as the day went on.

Shortly after noon rebels climbed the hill above town and raised a large Confederate flag, firing off a defiant volley. When the banner was seen from the street Union men quickly organized and armed themselves, stormed the hill and tore it down. Although some shots were fired in the melee, more were downed in the saloons. There were no fatalities but bitterness and resentment lasted for years. Lest anyone forget the incident the bluff, actually part of the rim rock above town, was named "Rebel Hill."

At the time of the party on the hill Col. Henry E. Dosch was on his way to Canyon City from St. Louis, Mo. Born in Germany June 17, 1841, and arriving in St. Louis in 1860, he lived there less than a year when he enlisted in the Union Army. By way of California young Dosch arrived at The Dalles on the Columbia River in 1864. There he set up an enterprise to pack supplies into roaring Canyon City. In later years, after he became a prominent citizen of Portland with a road named for him, he wrote an account of his adventure along the old Military Road in Eastern Oregon.

His partners John Snively and William Claffin furnished the money, Dosch wrote, and he the experience gained on his trip north. The packers carried about $25,000 worth of supplies to the camp, selling them at double the cost. "We didn't include flour in this, selling the staple which everyone must have, at cost—55 cents a pound. Nobody got rich but we made wages." The return load paid better. Canyon City gold was exceptionally pure without the infusion of copper that reduced value elsewhere. At $17 per ounce Dosch's pack animals were most attractive to road agents.

At this time Grant County had just been organized, the first election naming W. L. Laird as county judge and Tom Brents county clerk. After a short term the latter was replaced by saloon keeper Mike Goodwin and Dosch relates, "Mike didn't know the first thing about the duties required, so he named me as his deputy. I took over his job and served under C. H. Miller who had been elected county judge."

He refers to Cincinnatus Heine Miller who came across the plains in a covered wagon in his early teens. After a short stay with his parents he began a wandering career, fighting briefly in the Modoc War, traveling to the gold camps of northern California. As a youth of about eighteen he found life among the Digger Indians of the McCloud River country near Mt. Shasta very much to his liking because of the amiable Indian girls so easily available.

Going native, he shed his regular clothes for the fringed buckskins he was to affect during much of his life. Flitting from one acquiescent squaw to another he settled down with one whose "flowing hair," he wrote, "only partially screened the rounded young breasts of maidenhood." His white friend Jim Brock wrote later, "I should say a man would be crazy to live with one of them . . . the sight and smell of most would turn the stomach of any but a poet."

Of Miller's dalliance was born a daughter whom he named Cali-Shasta, then deserted both mother and child. Later he returned for the little girl and put her in the care of a friend in San Francisco. Moving to Eugene, Oregon, he worked on a newspaper which soon went out of business because of the editor's Confederate sympathies.

Some time later Miller and white wife Minnie and their small child joined a pack train for Canyon City, some of the animals carrying fruit trees, berry vines and ornamental shrubs. In the rough mining camp the family settled down in a cabin and Miller began writing the poetry that would bring him world fame. Dosch wrote of Miller, "He was an ardent admirer of Lord Byron, even affecting his idol's slight limp caused by a deformed foot. He wore his hair down to his shoulders and wore high boots, one of which was usually covered by a pant leg, the other leg being tucked inside. He loved to be conspicuous." Dosch, who often had to share the same office, complained that "Miller would often corner me so he could read me his stuff which I didn't much care for. I thought his wife Minnie wrote better, though her verses were never published."

But much of Miller's was, some of it in the Dalles *Times-Mountaineer*, sent out under a pen name—John Smith, Jr. Emboldened by success Miller submitted more material to his home town paper, the *Blue Mountain Eagle*, under his real name, Cincinnatus Heine Miller.

His marriage, ill-starred from the beginning, was dissolved and he moved to Portland where he continued his writings under a name that would be permanent—Joaquin Miller. Then came a European tour and in England his spectacular garb and flamboyant air "made a big hit," Dosch records. In 1907 Miller returned to his Canyon City home as a celebrity and there wrote "A Royal Highway of the World," actually a form of "letter to the editor." It was reproduced many times and sent to Grant and Harney County papers, commissioners and any other authorities he could think of. It protested the condition of the road from Canyon City to Burns. Miller claimed the "highway" was so clogged with brush that stage drivers had to carry axes and saws and cut their way through.

The road, now part of U.S. 395, is a modern paved highway, full of sharp curves as it skirts scenic Strawberry Mountain and many narrow canyons. It was formerly termed "Joaquin Miller Highway" but now the designation does not appear on maps.

MAIN STREET of Canyon City shows plunder taken by market hunters. Birds beaten out of swarming marshes bordering some sections of John Day River were ruthlessly slaughtered, even rare swans. Hunters pose with guns, butcher in apron. (Courtesy Oregon Historical Society).

THE RABBITS ALMOST HAD IT

Narrows, Oregon

In the sparsely populated area south of Burns the now defunct village of Narrows was built on an unusual site, unusual in that the two lakes between which it lies are twins except that one contains fresh, potable water, the other being brackish and undrinkable.

One of the lakes, its French name "Malheur" meaning "evil hour" since early day trappers discovered there a valuable cache of furs stolen by natives or other trappers, is fed by fresh water from Donner und Blitzen River. It appears this stream was crossed by a troop of cavalrymen en-gaged in the Snake Indian War in 1864, a furious electrical storm raging at the time and leader Col. George B. Curry gave it an apt German name.

Harney Lake is by nature isolated from any supply of fresh water, receiving only scanty rainwater and in times of flood a supply from its twin Malheur which overflows into a channel connecting the two. Harney's water, its salts gradually concentrated by evaporation, has become unusable for any purpose.

In 1892 on the narrow strip of land Charles A. Haines built a home centering a cattle ranch he hoped to establish. The single house turned out to be the nucleus for a good sized town because of its isolated position, the only stopping place in a vast lonely land south of Burns and north of Frenchglen where famed Peter French had his domain.

Haines put up several buildings to serve travelers in the otherwise uninhabited 80 miles of desert. In five years the settlement required a post office, in a few more a hotel, several saloons, livery stable and gambling house. A large store did a good business in merchandise brought by freight wagons from Burns. One oldtimer in the area, a rancher from Happy Valley recalls, "I was born at Narrows. It wasn't that my parents were living here, there was a midwife in the place and where else could a woman go to have a baby in this country?"

The only boom or rush Narrows had was on the side of the rabbits. The story is well remembered by Ray Novotny, county extension agent. There were always plenty of rabbits around but during the '20s not particularly troublesome to ranchers.

SCHOOLHOUSE from rear with corner of stone jail visible, about all left of Narrows' town center. No forest exists in this arid section except sparsest growth of junipers, few seen in right distance.

DESERTED SCHOOLHOUSE stands alone on treeless plain. Only family now living at Narrows is that of property owner, Henry Church, whose father came here in 1916. "I was a student in that schoolhouse until 1941," he says. "I was only in the fifth grade then but they had to close the school for lack of pupils."

Then unexplainably there was a population explosion among the long-eared, long-geared jacks. They made such inroads of forage and crops that the county placed a five cent bounty on each pair of rabbit ears brought in. Not in the habit of bothering much about such small game, ranchers now found some profit in shooting the pests and on the next trip to Burns collecting the bounty. Some, with only a few dozen pairs to turn in, were glad to do business with the Narrows storekeeper who paid three cents a pair in trade and who collected a nickel in Burns. When the depression came its effects seemed to extend even to the Narrows rabbits, keeping population down to a minimum.

Other fauna fared better. Both Malheur and Harney Lakes are bordered by lush growths of aquatic plants. From pre-historic times immense flocks of water birds have bred in thickets of reedy growths. Migratory fowl including herons, pelicans, egrets and geese gathered in such flocks as to temporarily obscure the sun. In 1908 the area just south of Narrows was set aside and dedicated by President Roosevelt as the Malheur Migratory Bird Refuge, the original area later expanded to 159,872 acres.

In the 1930s the road to Burns was paved and nearly all the ranchers around Narrows owned cars. They drove handily to the larger town to find more variety in the stores and Narrows was as good as doomed, its demise conceded when the hotel burned down.

Henry Church and his family are now the only residents. He owns the property adjoining the bird refuge, raising cattle on the vast acreage. The Churches live in a picturesque old house in the middle of the deserted town. They are interested in antiquities and during the last 20 years have uncovered over 100 arrowheads and other Indian artifacts around the farm. An obsidian knife they found was checked out at the University of Oregon which established its age as about 1000 years. Almost certainly the material came from Glass Buttes deposits of obsidian not far west of Burns.

The Churches find that owning a ghost town has its drawbacks. Some visitors have displayed a regrettable lack of respect for private property. When interviewed in 1966 by Robert Olmos, Portland *Oregonian* writer, Church said, "People have damaged and almost carried off the old buildings. I put up no trespassing signs in self-defense, but they are ignored, so I have had to tear down some of the old houses and expect to raze the rest."

PONDEROSA PINE is familiar tree in Ochocos, intricate textural pattern of plated bark shown here.

SOLIDLY BUILT JAIL, only stone building in Narrows. Not far from jail Mrs. Church found nearly buried Colt pistol. Although stock was rotted away serial number 107335 is still clearly visible.

STAGE LINE BLUES

Mitchell, Oregon

It did not take long for Canyon City to boil over after the news of the gold discovery spread east and west. There were no facilities for the people who thronged the place, no way for mail to get there. A mail route was a prime necessity and one was hurriedly established from The Dalles on the Columbia River, mainly over ancient Indian trails, twisting over flats and hills.

Mail was put in tightly strapped saddle bags. Daring riders carried letters at 50 cents each, newspapers, even though outdated, at $1. Some riders were waylaid and killed by Indians but dangers were accepted as part of the job.

Dust and nuggets in the veritable flood of gold from Canyon City were shipped to Portland by way of Sherar's Bridge and over the Barlow Road, or to The Dalles by the mail route. As Indian attacks along the way became more acute, the Federal Government improved the latter route to expedite the movement of soldiers to base camps and it was thenceforth called The Dalles-Canyon City Military Road.

Pony express and pack train were soon followed by regular stage lines, the first one operated by the man for whom Wheeler County would be named, Henry H. Wheeler. On May 1, 1864, he placed stock, wagons and coaches on the 180-mile run between the Columbia River town and the gold camp in the John Day Valley. Later he often related the next four years were the most exciting ones of his life.

Wheeler's first trip conveyed 11 passengers to Canyon City, about as many on the return, each paying a fare of $40. Then regular trips three times a week were established, Wheeler driving his rig with four horses. In 1865 he was awarded the mail contract. Encounters with Indians were varied and frequent, enough of them, Wheeler said, to fill a book, one in particular being a bloody hair-raiser.

On Sept. 7, 1866 he was driving the route between Dayville and Mitchell, accompanied by H. C. Page, Wells Fargo agent. Among the valuables were the usual mail, $10,000 in greenbacks, $300 in coin and several diamond rings. Near Mitchell a band of about twenty Indians appeared on horseback, opening fire almost at the same instant, the first bullet going through both of Wheeler's cheeks and taking out several teeth with a section of jawbone. Unable to speak he signaled Page to hold the Indians at bay as long as possible and jumping to the ground he managed to unhitch the horses. Then the two mounted a pair of animals never before ridden and got away to the road house at the Meyers ranch.

After Wheeler's wounds were dressed, he and Page returned to the scene of the attack to find the mail bags ripped open and contents scattered about. Valueless to the Indians they had strewn the greenbacks to the winds. Except for a small part of the currency all valuables including rings were recovered.

One of the several stopping places along the Military Road was named for J. H. Mitchell, former U.S. Senator from Oregon. By the time the place became large enough to be platted it already had two stores, blacksmith and hotel. Its location was not chosen but happened to be a good camping place. A stream called Bridge Creek afforded year around water and cottonwood trees shaded the small level area. The fact that the spot was at the bottom of a narrow canyon coming out of

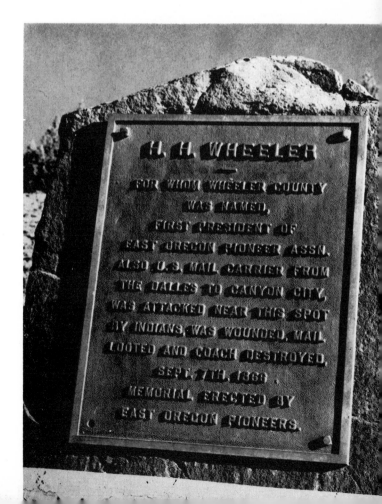

BRONZE PLAQUE marks site of stage driver Wheeler's most notable encounter with Indians.

DOORWAY to old homestead cabin near Mitchell.

barren mountains was overlooked while the town grew.

In the summer of 1884 Mitchell was flourishing, its many buildings crowded into the narrow confines of the canyon mouth. The season produced numerous heavy thunderstorms in the nearby mountains and one of them dumped a deluge concentrating in a tributary to Bridge Creek canyon. Ignoring the small watercourse at the junction, a nine-foot wall of water burst over a cliff and inundated the town. Damage was tremendous in proportion to the size and isolated situation. Entire buildings were carried away, the street covered with several feet of mud, boulders and debris. This flood, the first in a disastrous series, failed to take any lives. Having made such an ominous roar in going over the cliff all residents were warned and able to escape.

In 1904 another and even worse flood hit the community, sending down a thirty-foot wall of water that took out a total of twenty-eight buildings and killed two citizens. Phil Brogan, well-beloved historian of his area, writes in *East of the Cascades*, "Those who escaped to the hills watched the heavens blaze with lightning and heard the crash of thunder echoing from cliffs that were once ocean ooze." Most recent was a disastrous flood about 1960.

Calamitous fires were added to the unusual drama of Mitchell's existence. One blaze on March 25, 1896, destroyed nine buildings and ten more were lost in August of 1899.

Although the days of gold and pony express are long since finished, Mitchell did some rebuilding from destruction time and again, and still lives. Strategically located on U.S. 26 it provides supplies for far-flung ranches and gas for the traveler between Willamette Valley points and Eastern Oregon and Idaho.

BUILDINGS dating from Mitchell's early days of gold and stage coaches are few. This one of stone survives a few feet back of the row of main street stores. Solid metal door attests its use as a vault in early days Canyon walls rising directly behind gives hint of narrowness.

FAST DECAYING REMNANTS of barn in Ochoco Mountains above Mitchell shakily survive elements. Gate post, well rubbed by stock, is near collapse.

THE RIVER WAS A CHALLENGE

Sherar's Bridge, Ore.

In 1826-7 Peter Skene Ogden took an exploring party down the long miles of arid territory east of the Cascade Mountains, a major portion of "Oregon." One large river he encountered, tumbling in falls and rapids most of its length, was termed by the French Riviere aux Chutes and Riviere des Chutes, and by Lewis and Clark, the Clark. Ogden wrote of his crossing, "On Thursday September 26 we reached the River of the Falls and found an Indian camp of about 20 families. Finding a canoe and a bridge made of slender wood, which we began crossing, 5 horses were lost through the bridge."

Years later, John Y. Todd, whose father, John Y., built the first substantial bridge over the cataract, wrote, "It is difficult to believe that there could have been much of a bridge there when Peter Skene Ogden crossed it. It seems as if Ogden must have been blinded by the snow, because it is hard to think the Indians could possibly have built a structure that would support a horse."

The first John Y. Todd was born in Missouri, Nov. 30, 1830. Determined to join the forces going overland to fight the war with Mexico in 1846 and refused enlistment as being too young, he went along as driver of an ox team. Once in Mexico, however, young Todd was "drafted" as a regular soldier and returned to his home in Missouri in 1848, a veteran at 18.

When he heard the news of gold in California he went to the West Coast to try his luck at finding a bonanza. Denied this and depressed by summer's dry heat in the gold country, he went to San Francisco and boarded a steamer for Portland. At Astoria he was transferred to the steamboat *Lot Whitcomb* (see *Tales the Western Tombstones Tell*).

He sold wheat harvesting machinery up and down the Willamette Valley for several years and then turned Indian fighter, joining the Yamhill Company which attempted to subdue the Yakimas. After that the young Missourian went into the cattle business and eventually settled in Oregon's Tygh Valley on the eastern flank of Mount Hood.

Some pioneer wagon trains bound for the Wil-

OLD PHOTO gives hint of town-like settlement at crossing, no trace of Indian fishing village which developed more recently. After Todd built first bridge in 1860 most weary immigrants abandoned dusty Oregon Trail, taking short cut by way of Grass Valley and the Wamic approach to Barlow Road over Cascade Mountains. Location is narrowest defile in entire course of Deschutes River, deeply cut channel crowding river into black, swirling torrent rather than white rapids and cascades generally characteristic of river. Tolls of $3.75 for each yoke of oxen or team of horses plus $1 for driver were charged. Users beside immigrants were miners or freighters passing to and from Canyon City and John Day gold mines.

lamette Valley and nearing the goal, chose the Columbia River route for the last push. Others pressed on by land and encountered several difficult river crossings, the tumultous Deschutes by far the worst. Todd saw he could help his fellow pioneers and make money at it so in 1860 he built a bridge over the stream at a point where it deepened and narrowed between waterfalls.

For two years the bridge served well, then came a winter of heavy snows in the nearby mountains and hard spring rains which caused severe flooding, a surge in the Deschutes carrying away the span. Since Todd had put all his money into his buildings and logs necessary for rebuilding would have to come from mountain forests as before, he was forced to take in two partners, Ezra Hemingway and Robert Mays, before he could build a new bridge. When the new firm was organized and second span built, Hemingway bought out the other two and shortly, in 1871, sold out to a man named O'Brien who in turn sold to Joseph Sherar, the bridge bearing his name since.

Born in Vermont in 1833, Sherar also arrived in the West via the California mines, his digging done in the northern section and later the John Day mines of eastern Oregon. He saw in the bridge far greater opportunity for investment than had Todd and the other owners. Paying only $7,040 for the structure itself, he invested $75,000 in building approaching roads. Then he put up a stage station which soon developed into a 33-room hotel, large and elaborate for those primitive parts.

In 1868 a post office was established at the site with Hemingway as postmaster and now Sherar improved the building to succeed him. In addition to hotel and postal facilities the location had a store, livery stables and many other buildings.

MODERN "SHERAR'S BRIDGE" is part of State Highway 216. No trace exists of village once established here for early immigrants to Oregon Country. Instead large but transitory Indian village stands along both banks. Existing only during salmon runs, settlement consists of habitations ranging from stinking, garbage-surrounded tent shacks to luxurious campers. Indian fishermen erect temporary and seemingly precarious platforms suspended above water from which they wield long-handled nets. Salmon are particularly vulnerable here while resting after leaping falls just below and before ascending equally difficult one immediately above.

SEVERAL BUSINESS PLACES lined side of solid block in Campo Seco, one Adams Express Co., its two-story front still standing. At right, out of picture, is Esperson Building—at left are shown ruins of miners' supply house and general store. Still evident are dressed stones framing doors, windows of sandstone, rougher construction of meta-andesitic agglomerate, the common field stone of local area. Tree is ubiquitous "Tree of Heaven," seeds of which were brought over by Chinese, spread over much of West. View is from "backyard."

California

THE RIVER WAS FULL OF GOLD

Camp Seco, Calif.

Oregon City, California? No mistake. It was rough and tumble mining camp during early years of the great gold rush to the Mother Lode. Among the first outsiders reaching the strip coursing 150 miles along the lap of the High Sierra were Oregonians barely settled after crossing the plains to the Willamette Valley. Oregon so stimulated them they carried to many gold camps names like Oregon City, Oregon Creek, Oregon Hill and there were several Oregon Gulches, one bisecting a shallow valley not far from the Mokelumne River which was "full of gold."

The population of Oregon City quickly grew

VIEW, looks directly through ruins of store buildings adjoining Adams Express Co. Stones used in construction were undressed but some care was used in selecting flat surface for facing cut. Roofs have long ago disappeared. Walls get wet in winter to permit growth of grasses on top edges and long, hot summers dry them to sere, yellow state.

more cosmopolitan, news of riches there attracting men from other areas. Mexicans from Sonora were very numerous along the gold-flecked trail they called Veta Madre. Sonorans soon outnumbered Oregonians and deploring a lack of water, they gave the place a new name, Campo Seco or dry camp.

By 1854 the town had three hotels, many saloons, a brewery and that year a disastrous fire which razed all wooden buildings. With placer gold still flowing and a shallow hard rock mine nearby, inhabitants felt justified in building new hotels, rebuilding saloons and refurbishing stone structures, one the office of the Adams Express Co.

But prosperity had only a year or so to go before it sagged. Placer gold was then exhausted and the quartz veins were pinching out. A few people

moved away, a store closed and almost unnoticeably Campo Seco headed for ghostdom. Then somebody uncovered a deposit of copper nearby, a protruding piece of native, almost pure, copper.

The value of copper, always fluctuating, reached a high point in 1860. A newly organized group of financiers called Penn Copper Co. bought options on the property and soon had a big operation in full swing, gold almost forgotten. From then until about 1924 the fortunes of the dry diggings went up and down according to the price of copper.

In the early 1920s a group of eleven San Francisco Bay communities in need of water united to form the East Bay Utility Co., with the objective of placing a dam across the Mokelumne River to form a long reservoir above. Flood waters would cover many river bars that had yielded millions in

FRAME BUILDING, one of few in Campo Seco. Originally a saloon, some signs of old bar still evident inside, later a meat market, one old picture showing dim outline of steer's head on false front. Still later, contemporary with building of nearby Pardee Dam, enterprising merchant made oblong opening at near end, served drinks to construction workers, some soft by law, most spiked or neat "white mule" by demand.

BELOW BUTTE PEAK, high, conical mountains visible for miles around, is site of Butte City now represented by only solid structure built there. Basin, 1½ miles south of Jackson, was early discovered to be rich in gold, causing immediate growth of town built almost entirely of adobe and wood. One exception is this structure of Calaveras schist fieldstone with doors and windows of fired brick built by Xavier Benoist in 1854. Upper window spaces and ground level doors were fitted with iron shutters, familiar to Mother Lode visitors. After some years Benoist sold out to one Ginnochio whose name relic bears today. Store was built near old trail and when State 49 was put through it stood so close to edge passing cars almost brushed fenders. Then thieves stole heavy iron doors so conveniently close. State erected sturdy cyclone fence with several strands of barbed wire at top to protect historic building against further vandalism, an unsightly but effective barrier. Only other evidence of one time teeming town is cemetery above where bodies of many nameless miners lie.

gold and the corporation was forced to buy many dead claims at inflated prices set when rumors of the project reached the owners.

As work began hundreds of workmen poured into construction camps near old Campo Seco and suddenly a new enterprise sprang up—moonshining. After work laborers came in droves clamoring for something to drink with more authority than near beer. All right, said some Campo Secoans, we'll give it to 'em. They set up a still and shop in one of the old stone buildings, the illicit drink emporium never raided by prohibition agents and flourishing until the Pardee Dam was completed in 1930. Then, according to local legend, the operators of the traffic who had prudently continued to pay insurance premiums, set fire to the wooden interior of the stone building and faded out of history.

TINY CITY PARK honors Mark Twain. Gate is formed of mining relics such as ore car overhead.

RABBITS MADE HIM RICH

Angel's Camp, Calif.

Beside a name which strained credulity Bennager Rasberry had a worked-out placer claim, a cranky old muzzle loading shotgun and he was hungry. The rocky rises around Angel's Camp supported a lot of jackrabbits and if the miner could not find gold he could spend time gnawing away on the stringy meat of those sagebrush broncos.

Rasberry shot several and then had trouble with the ramrod. It was jammed in the barrel tightly and neither curses nor muscles could get it out. Losing his temper completely he fired the weapon at a rock a dozen feet away. The ramrod came out right enough and Rasberry saw it had scuffed off the weathered crust of the rock and exposed the yellow gleam of gold.

It may be assumed Mr. Rasberry forgot all about rabbits since it is recorded he picked up nuggets to the value of $700 before it got dark. Come daylight he returned with pick and shovel and that day returned with $2,000. When the following day's work netted $7,000 from the vein he made up his mind he had a gold mine and filed claim to it. Bennager Rasberry soon became the richest man in town and his name is perpetuated in an Angel's Camp street called Rasberry Lane.

George Angel was a veteran of the war with Mexico and went with other footloose, gold-hungry ex-soldiers to the Sierra foothills. He found a likely spot to camp on the bank of a small creek tributary to the Stanislaus but he also found throngs of other hopeful prospectors already working the gravels. Playing it safe, he set up a trading post before picking up shovel and gold pan. So although mining proved a spare time sideline for Angel, he was still able to sift out as much as ten ounces of gold on a good day.

The men Angel joined at the location that would bear his name proved to be the advance guard of the big rush. In those first months every man was friend with an equal chance and there was no need for formal claims. But when reports of the rich harvest reached the outer world and hordes descended on the peaceful community many a prospector found "a snake in his tent." When the solid citizens caught strangers working their favorite locations there was trouble and some killings resulted. Civilization had arrived and it became necessary to legalize claims. Yet this period, loosely called the "Age of Innocence," quickly came to an end when the creek sands gave up the last of the gold flecks.

By 1855 Angel's Camp was "law abiding" with wrong doers duly arrested by a legally appointed sheriff, tried in regular court proceedings varied according to the crime. At least this was supposed to be the procedure and sometimes it did work out that way. Among variations was the case of a miner killing another who called him a "hog thief." Although he had "sort of borrowed" the pig in question, he said, and although he had "et some of it," the slur had irked him to the point of drawing his gun and killing the porker's legal owner.

Some Angel's Campers thought the culprit should be strung up pronto and when lynching rumors spread the law sent to nearby San Andreas for aid in protecting the prisoner, at the same time rushing trial procedure. To a packed courtroom came the word that the San Andreas sheriff and emergency posse were nearing Angel's Camp. As if by pre-arrangement each court officer was seized and bound, the prisoner hustled to the hanging tree and was dangling from the end of a rope when the horsemen of the law rode up.

Today Angel's Camp is better known to the tourist than almost any other town in the Mother Lode. And this is not due to George Angel or the muzzle-loader of Bennager Rasberry or to any other bit of verified history, but to an incident nothing more than trivial, if indeed it happened at all.

The area around Angel's Camp was a hotbed for California folklore, nurturing over-fertilized stories about Joaquin Miller, Black Bart, salacious doggerel by anonymous miners and more classic tales by Bret Harte and Mark Twain.

It was in 1865 that Twain toured the Southern Mines. By that time they were "decaying" as a contemporary critic wrote it and it would seem the humorist found little of interest in the mines themselves, preferring, in Angel's Camp, the salubrious atmosphere of the Angel's Hotel bar. It is legend that bartender Ben Coon related to him a local anecdote which Twain jotted down in his notebook—"Coleman with his jumping frog. Bet stranger $50. Stranger had no frog and C. got him one. In meantime stranger filled C's frog full of buckshot so couldn't jump. The stranger won." Twain wove the fragments into a story which he later called a "villainous backwoods sketch" but which was printed and reprinted across the country and beyond in several languages.

$40,000 NUGGET

Carson Hill, Calif.

They were fifteen feet down, four Americans and a Swiss, working their claim at Carson Hill in the Mother Lode country of California. Darkness was falling but the men kept on digging and shoveling and rubbing the dust out of their eyes. Suddenly one of them, generally thought to be Perkins, struck a rock. Failing in an attempt to heave it out of the hole he decided to look at it closer in better light. He could thank his lucky stars he did. It was a big gold nugget. Taken down to Stockton, weighed on the Adams Express Company scales, the chunk of gold made the newspapers all across the land, reports giving the weight as anywhere from 141 pounds to 214 pounds, 8 ounces, depending upon avoirdupois and troy weight plus enthusiasm. In time the true weight was established at 195 pounds.

Mr. Perkins came from Lexington, Kentucky, to the gold fields at the first word of discovery. After mining a few years he still had never owned more than $200 in gold dust at one time but he had joined with four others and still had hopes. The men panned all available gold from their creek at Carson Hill and were working up the lode from which the placer gold had apparently come. They were doing fairly well on that fateful November 29 day of 1854 and were reluctant to knock off but after finding the big rock it is to be assumed they did.

The record does not state how big an argument there was over ownership of the nugget but it was decided that since Perkins owned the biggest share of the claim he was the "principal owner." So he and a fellow miner started for New York with their prize. Neither got that far at that time. At some point along the journey a New Orleans man offered Perkins $40,000 for the nugget which he accepted and promptly dropped from history. The

MONUMENT stands on bank of Stanislaus River at site of almost vanished Melones, first called Slumgullion, now camp ground operated by owners of nearby tavern. This operates in one of the few buildings remaining from days of ferry and gold camp. First miners, Mexicans from Sonora, claimed to have found nuggets like the seeds of "Melones."

DETAIL at entrance to wine cellar of James Romaggi house at Albany Flat, built 1852.

ROBINSON'S FERRY
STATE REGISTERED LANDMARK No. 276

IN 1848 JOHN W. ROBINSON AND STEPHEN MEA
ESTABLISHED FERRY TRANSPORT FOR FREIGH
ANIMALS AND PERSONS ACROSS RIVER. IN 185
HARVEY WOOD PURCHASED INTEREST AND LATE
ACQUIRED PROPERTY WHICH WAS MAINTAINE
BY WOOD FAMILY UNTIL 1911. CHARGES WER
50 CENTS FOR EACH PASSENGER, HORSE, JENN
OR OTHER ANIMAL.

MARKER PLACED BY CALIFORNIA CENTENNIALS COMMISSI
BASE FURNISHED BY ANGELS CAMP LIONS CLUB
DEDICATED MAY 22, 1949

THIS BUILDING is one of best preserved and most elaborate in Mother Lode. Pictured in several early publications it is variously termed "Romaggi Fandango Hall" and "Romaggi Adobe." Originally, at least, it was erected as home for James Romaggi, an Italian preferring grapes to gold and setting out vines and fruit trees, nearly duplicating green slopes in homeland. Appellation "Romaggi Adobe" is baffling since walls are constructed of selected, coursed slabs of amphibolite schist. One old photo shows badly weathered roofs of boards, doubtless once covered with shakes or shingles. Nearby road led to Los Muertos, scene of several battles between Mexicans and Americans in fall of 1852.

record follows the mass of gold to New Orleans where it was deposited in the Bank of Louisiana. It was later sold, the new owner taking it to Paris and exhibiting it as the largest nugget ever taken out of California or the United States. Which perhaps it was.

There have been no huge nuggets of gold reported for a long time but during the last half of the 19th century big chunks were being found all over the world, hysterically announced in the press as being the largest wherever found, either by weight or value. The word "nugget" is thought to be derived from "ingot," defined as any lump of pure metal cast into a particular shape. While a natural chunk of metal, specifically gold, is termed a nugget, it need not be pure metal but could include any amount of the matrix from which it came. Those found in California usually included some quartz as in the case of the Carson Hill find. The famous Welcome nugget found some years later in Australia and roughly the same bulk as the California one, was all gold and therefore holds first place.

There were many other lucky finds on Carson Hill, a man named Hance taking out a 14 pound lump of gold lying at the top of the hill. Scattered around and on Carson Hill were the rich Morgan mine, the Reserve, South Carolina, Stanislaus and others totaling a fantastic yield of $2,800,000 in gold during the most productive year, 1850. Little wonder mining authorities term Carson Hill the "classic mining ground of California." Ironically the man who made the original find and for whom the hill was named shared in little of the wealth produced there.

James S. Carson was a sergeant in Col. Stevenson's New York Volunteers and when the regiment was disbanded at the end of the Mexican War he was stranded in Monterey, California, with many other soldiers. With the news of James Marshall's discovery of gold in the race of Sutter's Mill, Carson joined a company of ninety-two men, mostly ex-soldiers, going to the gold fields. In the party were some who would leave their names for posterity in the Sierra foothills. The Murphy brothers

headed northeast to found Murphy's Camp. George Angel left his mark on a camp later celebrated as the home of Mark Twain's Jumping Frog and Carson, called "Captain," staked his claim and settled down to panning the creek sands, in ten days recovering 180 ounces of gold to excite all members of the party.

They scattered to locate claims but Carson became ill with "rheumatism" or some affliction which incapacitated him. After many months in bed he went back to the creek but again was taken sick, this time even more seriously, and was removed to Stockton. Recovering long enough to be elected to the state legislature from Calaveras County, he was making plans to return to his claim when he was stricken with his final illness. While he lay in his bed millions of dollars' worth of gold were taken from his hill. He died at Stockton in near poverty in 1853.

ACTUAL TRACES of original buildings of Melones are hard to find. These disappearing stone ruins are secluded in grass, brush, few hundred feet from road. Photographed in very early morning light remains seem properly spectral.

JENNY LIND, on bank of Calaveras River, was busy place of over 400 a year after gold discoveries there in 1849, about three quarters being Mexican, Chinese miners. Town suffered from difficult access. In freshet of 1852 Calaveras was flooded to such depth supplies were brought by boat directly from Stockton, overloading stores and supply houses, many perishables spoiling. Stores usually provided bar along one side for customers, many buying more goods after pickup. Orango Brothers store had such a bar and known to be built of adobe, it could be one pictured here. Louis Rosenberg built stone and adobe clothing store nearby, advertising "Corect Attire For The Miner Or Prospector." Jenny Lind, named for singer who never got within 2,000 miles of town, had large Chinese section. Described as "crazily zigzagging rabbit burrows," motley collection of joss houses, opium dens, laundries extended one-half mile. Orientals were employed in stone quarries above town, hauling rocks in "China barrows," with bed slung on pivoting arrangement.

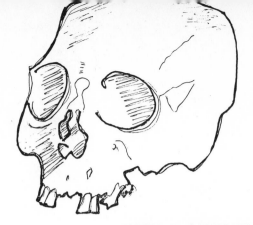

CALIFORNIA

THE LADY FOUND A SKULL

Mormon Bar, Calif.

Mrs. Ellison wanted to plant a garden. "The spot where I wanted to plant my tomatoes," she reported, "was hard and dry. I diverted the spring water to spread over it and let it soak overnight. Next day it was so easy to dig I got carried away and made the planting holes deeper than necessary. At the bottom of one I uncovered a bone that looked human to me. A little more digging uncovered a skull that I was sure was human."

It was but it did not belong to one of the Mormons who in 1849 settled here on the west side of Mariposa Creek, two miles southeast of the old Mariposa gold camp. Mr. and Mrs. Ellison bought property here in recent years and found very little evidence of Mormon occupation. The Saints panned what gold there was in the creek and moved on to richer fields.

The Mormon Bar area is neglected by historians. Technically the spot is not on the quartz seam constituting the Mother Lode proper. The one-time village does not show on maps of the California Division of Mines' book *Geological Guide Book* on the Sierran Gold Belt, these showing the still active town of Mariposa as the southern terminus. Nevertheless the country around and along lower Mariposa Creek was the center of seething activity for a few years.

Just to the west was Buckeye where James Savage had one of his trading posts. A short distance south was Ben Hur and Bootjack lay slightly east. All these shared in the transient prosperity of Mormon Bar. Ranches established here later were fenced by miles of stone walls skilfully erected by Chinese coolies in 1862, each required to put up a rod and a half daily or lose his job. He was paid

"six bits" a day, the Chinese contractor receiving $1.75.

Until a few years ago there was a visible Chinese cemetery here. The ruins of several adobe buildings marked the site and still more recently a small frame store, all described in current guides as being viewable relics. They are no longer there. Cemetery occupants were exhumed for shipment to the Orient to be reburied. Grass and brush make the site uniform with the landscape, the adobe ruins gone, the store razed a few years ago.

Intrigued with the skull she found Mrs. Ellison called in Francis A. Riddell, State Park Archeologist from Sacramento. He reported that all evidences indicated a large village once existed here, at least several hundred years before the advent of the whites. Present Mariposa Indians have no knowledge of their predecessors. Exact dates of older occupancy are unknown, no radiocarbon tests having been made. Says Riddell, "I found eight or ten burials and numerous arrowheads during the course of my four days of excavation at the site. More scientific work should be done here."

And Mrs. Ellison has the answer to that. She says many more artifacts than stated were found in her garden, such as beautiful abalone bangles, pottery bowls in good condition. When she objected to giving up these relics for classifying purposes work was abandoned.

SITE of prehistoric Indian village lies at Mormon Bar. Granite outcropping offered conveniently situated **metate**, this multiple version rather unusual. In these holes aborigines ground abundant acorns into coarse flour for food.

ALL'S NOT GOLD THAT GLITTERS

Knight's Ferry, Calif.

Well it was in the paper and they sent a reporter probably and he must have seen it . . . there—see the headline in the San Joaquin *Valley Republican?* "THE GREAT KNIGHT'S FERRY DIAMOND . . . here, I'll read it:

"The story goes that a party of miners were working a claim of sluice and hydraulic pipes at Buena Vista almost exactly opposite from Knight's Ferry. One night about dark a pipeman saw an object which he had washed out of the bank glittering on a pile of dirt and stones, about to be washed through the sluice. It's effulgent gleams lit up all the space in the vicinity, causing much astonishment to hardy workmen.

"The miner picked it up and moved along to show it to his comrades, but accidentally dropped it into the sluice where it was carried down by the current of the water into the mass of dirt and stones known as the tailings. A company of spiritualists from Knight's Ferry is now trying to locate the present locality of the jewel which is reported to be larger than the Koh-I-Noor."

All of which must have shown gold rushing settlers in California that newspapers were not just pulp and ink but human after all. With huge gold nuggets and gleaming yellow seams being uncovered every day since James W. Marshall discovered the first in the Sutter's Mill race January 19, 1848,

there was little headline value in ordinary gold finds. So, in the early 1850s the San Joaquin newspaper asked itself, why not jolt the public with a diamond discovery? Aw, it was all in fun, fellows.

In 1841 William Knight left Indiana with the Workman-Rowland party to become a farmer in California. He settled in the Sacramento Valley at a spot where the Sacramento River offered a natural landing place. Presumably he received a grant to the area, building a rude house on top of an ancient Indian mound termed by the natives "Yodoy." The shelter was of willow poles and reeds, tied with rawhide and plastered with mud. He established a crude ferry here and the location was called Knight's Landing.

On April 26, 1848, three months after Marshall's historic find, a San Francisco newspaper carried a story stating, "There are now about 4,000 white people, besides several hundred Indians, engaged in mining, and from the fact that no capital is required, they are working in companies on equal shares or alone as individuals . . . no other implement is required than an ordinary sheath knife to pick the gold from the rocks."

This decided William Knight to go to the Stanislaus River. It was one of the larger streams fed by Sierra snows and along its reach many early battles between Mexicans and Indians were fought, the war brought to a conclusion by a bloody clash in May of 1826. Leading the defeated natives was

EARLY SKETCH of Knight's Ferry shows suspension-type bridge apparently limited to foot traffic. Further upstream is another, possibly earliest covered bridge.

Chief Estanislao who was educated at Mission San Jose but turned renegade and incited his people to revolt. He lost his cause but his name is remembered in connection with one of the most romantic rivers in California's gold country.

The main road to Sonora, center of the Southern Mines, led from Stockton in the valley and crossed several streams of which the Stanislaus was the most formidable. Knight saw the difficulties the would-be miners were having and thought at once of the opportunity for a ferry. Instead of going on to the gold fields as intended he settled on the bank and put together a rude contraption that just did get the miners and baggage across.

He was able to be of service still further. Gen-erally called "Dr. Knight" because of some education in Indiana, he built a small shelter for an infirmary and gave simple first aid to prospectors suffering from exposure and hardships. Fees for this may have been negligible but ferry fees mounted to $500 a day at height of traffic.

Yet Knight was not able to enjoy his prosperity very long, dying suddenly on Nov. 9, 1849. New owners improved the ferry and river property, enterprising brothers Lewis and John Dent. They also erected a grist mill on the bank and then joined with others to span the river with a bridge.

It was built in 1854 and a second, some historians saying a duplicate of the first, being still in service, completed in 1862. There is confusion here

VENERABLE COVERED BRIDGE still stands secure, author's heavy pickup camper making several crossings in August of 1967. Question: did U. S. Grant have a hand in designing it? This view is made from ruins of grist mill, water in foreground from Stanislaus River coming through penstocks during flood earlier in year.

GRIST MILL erected by Dave Tulloch in 1862 with Englishman T. Vinson as supervising stone mason, after original was wrecked with first bridge by flooding Stanislaus River. Material is locally cut pink sandstone. Well built, structure was still almost intact in 1940s, has since deteriorated with complete loss of roofs.

as old pictures of the town show a suspension-type bridge. And authorities differ about the engineering aid credited to U. S. Grant. One usually reliable source claims Grant "helped draw plans for the second bridge in 1862" yet there was a Civil War raging at that time which fully occupied the general's attention in East and South.

Grant was at Knight's Ferry in 1854. He left Fort Vancouver Sept. 24, 1853, by lumber vessel for San Francisco on his way to Fort Humboldt, site of the present Eureka. While stationed there Grant made several trips to San Francisco where he could indulge in his hobbies, jousting with bottles and handling horses.

His wife Julia, left behind in the East, while Grant served cn the Coast, was a sister of the Dent brothers. Sometime during that 1854 summer Grant made a visit to them at Knight's Ferry, a resident reporting in a diary that the captain was seen on one occasion driving down the street in "a peculiarly jovial mood." In front of his buggy were three horses in single file and behind it three empty buggies. Several other such lively incidents are related with no mention of the bridge or of Grant's reputed aid in planning it.

Whoever the designer, this early span was slung too low to allow for such a flood as occurred in 1862 when it was carried away. With the bridge went the grist mill, receding waters leaving a fringe of sacked flour along the lower banks. It was said the contents were quite usable after an outer crust was removed.

MORE BULLETS FOR THE NORTH

Copperopolis, Calif.

The ledge of rock had a greenish-rust color but it sure didn't look to Hiram Hughes like there was metal in it. They said gold was where you found it and gold or silver was what he was looking for and, well, was there any left around here? It didn't seem so after all the digging around he'd done. Now that rusty looking rock—he sure would look like a danged fool taking some of that into an assay office. But what if he did? Only a gimlet-eyed metallurgist and a few Mexican loafers would know. Where's that chipping hammer . . . ?

Hiram Hughes was a Johnny-come-lately to the gold country, this Calaveras area on the Sierra's western slope, and he came here believing he just might find some of the yellow stuff overlooked by the others ahead of him. By 1858 most good or promising gold deposits had been located but Hughes while tardy was also persistent. After combing the Calaveras hills he worked north along the Mother Lode and into the Northern Mines. The next year found him in the Washoe silver region but he could find no trace of that white metal either.

So when he returned to Quail Hill where he spotted the greenish-rust colored rock, Hughes was about ready to quit looking for anything but a bottle of whiskey to help him forget all the hard work. But before he stopped in a saloon he took the chunk of rock to the nearest assay office. The report made him want to holler clear back to Kansas. The sample was nearly a third copper and worth $120 to the ton.

Just about this time another prospector, Thomas McCarty, made a similar discovery in the same area. He took as partners W. K. Reed, Dr. Blatchy and Thomas Hardy. The year was 1860, the country full of rumors that a civil war was about to explode and McCarty's discovery was named the Union Mine. In a few months the Keystone, Empire and Napoleon were added to the complex and a town called Copperopolis was growing up around it.

In 1863 W. K. Reed built a toll road, usually referred to as Reed's Pike, a rough trail over which ox teams hauled $1,600,000 in copper ore the first year. Although it had to go all the way to Wales to be smelted, the finished metal provided most of the copper needs of the Union Army during the war. And this gave Copperopolis, with a population of 10,000 a boom bigger than that in any of the gold camps nearby. When Reed sold out his interest in the Union, now the largest producing copper mine in the country, he got $650,000 for it. Shares in the mine, if sold by the foot, brought $200 for that much ground. During this period copper was worth an all time high of 55c a pound. Six mines were going full tilt and a railroad was being brought in from Stockton.

At the end of the war copper dropped to 19c and mines closed or curtailed operation. The Stockton-Copperopolis Railroad came to an ignominious end at Milton, about two-thirds of the way in and the place familiarly termed "Copper" was on the way out. In 1902 the Union reopened with a new smelter and 500-ton flotation mill. It produced varying quantities of copper with surges through the two world wars, then again closed. Since 1861 the mines produced 72 million pounds worth something over $12 million.

One hundred years after the big copper discoveries another product, asbestos, was located not far away. In 1960 Jefferson-Lake Sulphur Co. of Houston, Texas, paid $4,652,000 for a 500-acre tract on which to build a huge asbestos operation. This tremendous enterprise is not close enough to Copperopolis to mar the beauty and charm of the old copper camp.

LARGE STONE CORRAL near Copperopolis is one of several in area, this one of best preserved. Most were built by Chinese laborers during mining heyday.

Stop traveler and cast an e
As you are now, so once was
As I am now so you must be
Therefore prepare to follow me.
Prepare for death make no delay
I in my bloom was snatched awa
When death did call me to depar
I left my friends with acheing hear

CLASSIC EXAMPLE of "tombstone poetry" carved on marker in Copperopolis cemetery. Burial here was distinctly segregated into four sections—Masonic, I.O.O.F., Catholic and Protestant—separated by 4-foot stone walls.

BUSIEST SECTION of old Copperopolis during Civil War. Left was company warehouse, center building under old oak tree Copper Consolidated Mining Co. offices, right, one of most historic structures in California. Copper produced here was important to Union cause, regiment established to protect mines from possible Confederate sabotage. Soldiers used building as armory for entire period. When news of Pres. Lincoln's assassination reached town "Union Blues" assembled here and formed column on street in foreground, marching north several blocks to Congregational Church for services in honor of martyred war leader. In earlier gold camp of Columbia several brick buildings were torn down to expose rich ground for sluicing. Some salvaged bricks were used to construct this armory. Huge iron doors are considered largest in Mother Lode country.

IRON-DOORED JAIL is built of rough field stone. No path or trail now to structure. Luxuriant growth of several varieties of grasses form greensward in early spring but in August present barrier of bristly seeds that penetrate socks, shoes, to photographer's discomfort.

MARBLE STONE suggests question instead of identifying long-forgotten miner who rests here. Likely it is simply-marked foot-stone, strayed from more completely identifying head-stone.

SOLID BRICK BUILDING served as Union Mine warehouse in Civil War days. Small, frame, sheet-metal-covered structure was successively store, saloon, laundry, etc.

WALDO had several livery stables, all once facing old Kalispell Trail, this one half block from Krag Hotel.

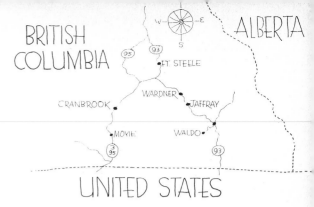

British Columbia

TAMING THE TALL UNCUT

Waldo, B.C.

If three men and their homes constitute a settlement, old Crow's Nest Landing was one, the spot a lonely one in 1905. W. W. Waldo, from south of the border, was one, owning a shack on the bank of the Kootenay River near the place where steamers from "down in the States" bound for Fort Steele could land at the muddy banks. The boats started at Jennings, Montana, with supplies hauled there by wagon. The other settlers were Jim Squiers and Newt Berry, famed horse ranchers, who had their home across the river from Waldo's. Many fine blooded horses came from their ranch.

In February of 1905 the brothers Hales H. and Joseph W. Ross came out to the Kootenay country from Whitemouth, Manitoba. They purchased a small sawmill from a company in Fernie to the north, installing it at the point where Elk River flows into the larger Kootenay. After operating it for a time the brothers looked around for a site to suit their fast growing ambitions, bought Waldo's property and began to develop the area as a sawmill town. Waldo returned to the States.

Next year the Ross brothers built a large sawmill near the river where lumber could be loaded on the S.S. *Waldo Belle*, just put into regular service. Many of the large frame buildings erected in the Kootenay country around 1907 were built with Ross Brothers' lumber from Waldo. When the Great Northern ran a line through there from Rexford, Montana, to the coal fields at Fernie and

Michel, the Canadian Pacific followed with a spur to Waldo. The wagon road was still a slightly improved Kalispell Trail, the old route from Montana to the gold camps of Fisherville, Wild Horse and later Fort Steele.

The Baker sawmill was the second large one in the town which thrived and grew yet never be-

GROUP OF EQUISETUM—mare's tail or scouring rush—lifted at site of long vanished Davis sawmill, brought to studio for photographing. Altho exquisitely proportioned, plants become invasive, pernicious weeds in gardens. Lovers of damp places, these "rushes" lived as giants 100' tall in marshes when world was young, fossilized remains constituting appreciable portion of most coal.

came a boom town. Dr. T. Saunders and his faithful nurse took care of all physical ills without the convenience of a regular hospital. Veterinarian Dr. Rutledge came regularly from Cranbrook to maintain the health of numerous horses used in the bush around the mills, also willing to make "house calls" in emergencies. One popular traveling man was "Whistling" Powell who came regularly in his chain-drive automobile to service sewing machines, a valuable effort in a community where no "store bought" clothing was available. And on one gala occasion an organ grinder came to Waldo, complete with a jaunty-capped monkey. Exciting too was a visit by a band of gypsies who camped in their covered wagons at the river. Children were fascinated by their fires burning most of the night and some adventurous adults had their fortunes told at the camp, for a fee of course. Then there was Mr. Rahal, the "jeweler," who periodically appeared in Waldo with two large leather packs on his back, selling watches, rings, cheap jewelry. He later established a conventional jewelry store in Fernie.

With the growth of the Ross brothers business, the partners took in another who had been an outside salesman, one Telford, from Saskatoon. He sold much lumber there and the sawmill name was changed to Ross-Saskatoon Lumber Co. Ltd. The two mills served the town until well into the 1920s when both closed down. Waldo, like other one industry communities, quietly disintegrated. Fires took out many buildings, leaving only a few like snaggle teeth along the old Kalispell Trail.

The railroad tracks have long since been torn up leaving lush pasturage and no stock to graze it. Down along the banks of the Kootenay River the famous mosquitoes of the region remain traditionally huge and vigorous. Crow's Nest Landing and Pigeon's Landing a mile upstream are now strictly for the birds.

KRAG HOTEL was one of the three in Waldo, this only remaining. Another, McConnell's, was used for hay storage for some years. Krag facade faces open meadows filled with blooming clover which formerly was main road thru town following old Kalispell Trail. Present road runs along rear. Nearby were tracks of long abandoned Great Northern line.
Beginning at right front was bar extending full length of north wall. Bartender Billy Palmer, one of four sons of owner, had long standing quarrel with fellow townsman Martin Heller and kept sawed-off shotgun under bar. One day Heller strode in suddenly and without giving Palmer chance to grab gun, shot him dead.
Immediately organized posse pursued murderer, overtaking him near Kootenay River bank. When Heller raised gun to fire at pursuers, posse members fired first, wounding him so severely he died on way to hospital. Story was related by one time resident, Douglas Ross, born at Waldo in 1909, now of Vernon, B.C.

AND INDIAN PETER GOT RICH

Moyie, B.C.

During the brief period Fort Steele was "occupied" by Northwest Mounties, commanding officer Major Sam Steele was able to conciliate the Indians of the Kootenay to the point where whites no longer felt the danger of a general uprising. The truce however was an uneasy one as far as native leader Chief Isadore was concerned.

Father Coccola and other priests from the mission established a short distance north in Mary's Valley had been working hand in hand with Major Steele to bring about a general peace. Since the Indians were suspicious of the strong combination, the departure of the Mounties actually helped smooth relations with the tribes, only Isadore remaining implacable. When Father Coccola tried to move him to the mission he replied, "No. You can even threaten me with attack by soldiers, but next spring I will plow my land as usual. I would rather die of bullets than by starvation." But by the fall of 1888, Isadore too was persuaded and total peace reigned.

It was true funds provided by the government helped sustain the mission school. Parents grudgingly acknowledged that children attending were "fat and healthy" but not all the adult Indians were so well looked after. When a hungry group of them came to Coccola for help one day the desperate priest made a suggestion. "Until we get enough money to help your people more fully, why don't your men go out in the hills to see if you can find a silver mine as some white men have been doing?"

Several Indians did exactly that. After a few weeks one native named Indian Pete returned to the mission to see Father Coccola in private. Alone with the priest he opened a little rawhide bag and took out a chunk of almost solid silver the size of an egg. The dazzled Coccola sent for James Cronin, a mining expert visiting at the mission. A small party was organized to go to the spot where the galena was found, Indian Pete leading the way. The vein ultimately became the famous St. Eugene silver mine at Moyie, at its height the largest producer in the country, in ten years yielding over $11 million.

The location was immediately developed under direction of the man who knew how to do it, technician James Cronin, one claim staked out to Indian Peter, the next to Father Coccola. When work began it was discovered the St. Eugene (Coccola) vein dipped into Peter's, all agreeing the two properties be worked as a unit. Deeper penetration in 1895 exposed a vein of silver-lead eight feet wide and it was obvious the mine was bigger than the priest could manage with small funds available. He sold out to financier John A. Fich of Spokane for $120,000, divided it with Indian Peter and returned to his mission.

The Indian bought a plot of good farm land, had a home and barn erected on it, stocked it with cattle, horses and sheep. Coccola spent his share on a fine new church, St. Eugene, at the mission and finished paying for the hospital previously constructed mostly on hope. There was enough left to care for and feed his parishioners for some time.

MAIN BUILDING, head frame of famous old St. Eugene workings. Overall production of $11 million is amazing in view of many difficulties, closures. Last activity lasted from 1911 to 1919. Ore contained 10 ounces of silver to 1 of lead with lesser amounts of zinc. Mine workings had 30 different levels, some upper ones penetrating deeply into mountain, lower ones extending under Lake Moyie.

FIREHOUSE built around 1900 still stands in Moyie at upper end of street. Characteristic of period is hose tower where wet hoses were hung to drain, dry out.

DUMPING MECHANISM detail on long-idled ore cart. Relic stands on old dumps just above Moyie Lake, partially visible in background left.

WILD DAYS IN THE BUSH

Fort Steele, Fisherville, Wild Horse, B.C.

It was the biggest Independence Day celebration held in Canada and very possibly the last. Montana liquor was flowing freely before July 4 and a good share of it into one Walker and "Yeast Powder" Bill. They agreed to disagree very violently and the crowd demanded a shoot-out. Bill's first shot went wild and Walker's first took Bill's thumb. This aggravated him mightily and he shot Walker dead.

Yankee prospectors smelling gold paid little heed to international boundaries in 1863. The story of how a party from notorious Hell Gate, Montana, founded a mining camp in British Columbia, would long ago have been forgotten but for a journalistic curiosity, the Fort Steele *Prospector*.

The long defunct paper was produced on a typewriter and reproduced by mimeograph. A complete file is owned by Basil G. Hamilton, of Invermere, B.C. The copy dated 18 April, 1896 begins: "The following facts relating to the early days on Wild Horse Creek have been learned from some of the old timers still living in the country."

The article tells of a half-breed named Findlay and two companions hailing from Frenchtown, fifteen miles northwest of Missoula, roaming the Kootenay country in hopes of finding placer gold. The men did discover a rich deposit in the shape of "pumpkin seeds" (perhaps the same type of nuggets called "melones" by Mexicans in Sierra streams. By late summer the party gleaned $700 worth of the little flat nuggets and with the first flakes of snow, packed up and headed for home, fearing to be trapped in the wild, inaccessible country.

They stopped at the Hudson's Bay post on the Tobacco Plains and found a buyer for their gold in the factor, a man named Linklater. Although the only white resident there he must have spread the news for the next spring several parties formed in the area and headed for the upper Kootenay country to search for Findlay's find.

Perhaps with inside information, one party of fifteen from Hell Gate found the place called Findlay Creek. It was still covered with snow and lacked pasturage for their mounts so the men retraced their tracks to a lower elevation where the

WINDSOR HOTEL was built in 1895 as Delgardno House by Robert D. Mather. Registers contain such illustrious names as Benjamin Harrison, Grover Cleveland, William McKinley, Sir William Laurier-Jones Skinflint, Paris, France(?). Present official status is as Fort Steele Historic Park. In early days building was encircled by fancy-trimmed balcony.
One year was enough for Northwest Mounted Police headed by Major Sam Steele to pacify disgruntled natives without aid of stockade or mounted guns. His tact and understanding receives most credit for success. Brief presence of Mounties was responsible for founding of busy town that survived as long as river traffic was most important means of transportation and gold was found in paying quantities.

grass was already several inches high. They all went to work in the creek, finding a little color and more as they worked upstream. Then they hit the bonanza, a deposit that kept them all busy right there, nobody going up to Findlay Creek even when the snow there melted. One man heard a sound on the bank, looked up from his pan to see a fine shiny black cayuse stud horse. "Stud Horse Creek," the place became.

Amounts of gold taken from the river are almost unbelievable. One claim alone, staked by Bob Dore, yielded $7,000 in a single day. Even ordinary days averaged $3,500. Yet the miners could not eat the gold. With unlimited resources food was so scarce some men almost starved. In the early spring of 1865 flour sold there for $1.25 a pound when it could be found, tobacco $15 and all else in proportion. Beef became unobtainable. A herd of sheep was driven in and they sold for 50c a pound on the hoof. Of a total summer population of 3,000, 800 miners wintered over. Drivers of the first trains with food supplies from the Flathead Mission in Montana found on May 15 only 400 men in camp, the others out hunting or fishing for food.

A year or two later found better conditions at the camp called Fisherville, after Jack Fisher, a prominent member of one of the first parties. In that first village a double row of log cabins was built almost on top of the first diggings and when it was found the best ground extended beneath them, Fisherville had to go. Without too much regret, as annual freshets had undermined them

anyway, the miners tore the buildings down as fast as digging advanced.

In the meantime a new town was going up on a higher bench above Stud Horse Creek. Miners thought it should be named after the creek but by now there was government of a sort, more or less under control of P. O. Reilly, Gold Commissioner. Said Reilly, "This will be a permanent city. Although we are a womanless community of 3,000 men, the ladies are bound to come in eventually. Think how embarrassing the name Stud Horse would be to them." His solution was a compromise acceptable to the majority, the less rugged "Wild Horse."

Although the new camp proved as transient as its predecessor, it is estimated hundreds of men were making $3,000 to $6,000, some up to $20,000, in the few months of good weather. Fisher's company with six partners took $1 million in 1865, Dore Company with ten, $150,000. Hundreds of nuggets here far exceeded the little pumpkin seeds, ranging up to a pound, one a giant of 32 ounces. As most of the miners were Americans an estimated total of $5 million was going to Walla Walla and Missoula. Again estimating, a conservative total of $17 million was harvested up to 1896.

In one of those big production years came the Fourth of July bust that found "Yeast Powder" Bill a murderer. Whatever his true name (some accounts call him "Yeast Porter" Bill) he got away, making camp near Brewery Creek where he was found asleep, rolled up in a blanket. Bob Dore pulled a gun on him and herded him back to town,

VERY OLD STORES strung along north side of road leading to Wild Horse Creek, mecca of trout fishermen. At extreme left is glimpse of ferry office, possibly oldest building in Fort Steele and typical of early log structures.
Larger complex was also by Galbraith brothers, replacing earlier log buildings in 1890s. Building with porch was store, in between saloon and right, hardware, feeds, livery stables. View looks northeast, road leading left into gulch of Kootenay River.

the miners electing a sheriff, judge and jury for trial purposes. It lasted only a few minutes, Y. P. Bill being acquitted on condition he leave the country forthwith. Not long after this Constable John Lawson was killed while attempting to arrest a horse thief named Brown who was later caught at a creek near Bonner's Ferry, Idaho, and slain, the creek still bearing the name Brown.

Wild Horse was the seat of government some twenty years, though without permanent officers of the law, circuit judges stopping at intervals to take care of accumulated cases of transgression. Gold mining gradually changed from panning the placers to deeper digging, then to hydraulic operations on a vast scale. When the yield became scanty the companies closed down and miners began to move away until in 1882 there were only eleven whites working their claims. Following the universal pattern, more easily satisfied Chinese then took over the placers.

One of the first miners here was John Galbraith who held land claims from Wild Horse Creek to the Kootenay River. In 1865 he decided to get out of the icy waters of the creek, obtaining a charter to operate a ferry across the river and run a pack train into the camp nearby. He opened a store on the river bank, established a post office next door and others came in to set up businesses. As a settled community it naturally took the name of Galbraith's Ferry. In 1874 brother Robert joined him and then took over John's interests to become a member of legislature representing East Kootenay.

Relations with the Kootenay Indians were on a steady if not cordial basis until 1884 when there was an incident that placed the whole country in danger and resulted in the founding of Fort Steele. Head of the Indian tribes was Chief Isadore. One of his men was charged with the murder of two white placer miners on the trail between Wild Horse and Deadman's Creek. A posse of miners overtook and captured the tribesman, Kapula, lodging him in the Wild Horse jail, less than seven miles from Galbraith's Ferry. Isadore and braves broke open the calaboose, took Kapula, the chief warning the provincial constable to get out of the country. Alarmed officials persuaded Isadore to return Kapula, promising him safe conduct at least until after the trial. Then they sent for Northwest Police, particularly Major Sam Steele.

Steele was the perfect man for the job, just and sympathetic to the Indian viewpoint. He came to Wild Horse, held a hearing of evidence from all concerned and decided the actual murderers of the miners were white renegades who blamed the Indian. Kapula was immediately freed and to further

BUILDING housed executive offices, constructed when Fort Steele was center of government for all East Kootenay. With decline of river town as metropolis, offices were moved to Cranbrook, building then reverting to use as hotel. Under protection now as relic it will be restored as government building.

cement relations, Steele arranged for establishment of Indian schools and agricultural aid. As a safety measure a fort was built on the arid elevated plain above Galbraith's Ferry and called Fort Steele.

Barracks buildings were constructed of yellow pine logs, partly hewn, sheeted and floored with common lumber, according to Major Steele's report. They had to be large enough to quarter a whole division without crowding. Stables for seventy-five horses had saddle and harness rooms under the same roof. There was a hospital 25 ft. x 40 ft., officers' quarters, guard room cells, casualty store and orderly room. In addition there were sergeants' mess, kitchen and staff sergeant's quarters, stores, horse shoeing and carpenter's shops and other structures. Steele included the note, "A sufficient quantity of beef, potatoes and fuel is obtainable here of good quality and reasonable prices. Twenty-two thousand pounds of oats have been purchased ... but the hay is of poor quality."

Interviewed for the *Daily Colonist* of January in 1963, was "Red" Nichol, then over 80 years of age. After serving in the Boer War he came to Fort Steele in 1902 and for more than 50 years served as big game hunter for parties from all over the world. When he came to the fort on the Kootenay River, he said, there were seven hotels with drinking and gambling freely flourishing in all. He remembered especially the Del Gardno, Windsor, Imperial, Fort Steele and Strathcona. "There were lots of wild women too, but we kept them all across the river." At the end of the interview Red was silent for a time, then concluded, "Fort Steele must be at its lowest ebb now. There isn't even a bootlegger left any more."

GAUNT BUILDING forms frame for most conspicuous peak in this part of Steeples Range, spur of Rocky Mts. Fisher Peak, 9,200,' retains some snow in sheltered ravines all summer. Mountain presents climbing problems. Ascent demands expert technique in rock work, first ascent made without technical aids by "Red" Nichol, big game guide for many years. He had rugged physical constitution to make up for lack of ropes, pitons.

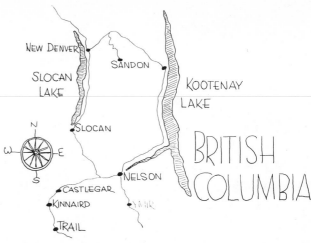

"IT WAS LIKE THIS, SON . . ."

Ymer, B.C.

"There was a lot going on when I first went to work as a miner here," the last old timer remaining in the former gold camp of Ymer (Wi-mer) told the author in 1965. "I was born on Prince Edward Island on June 9, 1882. My name is Alexander MacDonald, but why don't you just call me Alec?

"No, there never was any placering. Maybe once in a while somebody would find a little nugget in the creek, but it really was all hard rock mining. The man that found the lode was a Frenchman, he was a real geologist prospector, not the kind that goes around with a pan.

"The name of the town? Well the Frenchman named his mine the Ymer, so they called the town by that name. I don't know exactly, but if you want to go to the trouble to look through the Bible its there somewhere, the name of a Greek giant, I think.

"They built an 80 stamp mill up there on the hill next to the mine, it was the biggest stamp mill in the British Empire at that time and I think maybe since, too. Yes there were a few silver mines around here, but they weren't so much, you know. The Yankee Girl was the biggest, it was down there across the creek. You don't hardly ever find any gold without some silver, lead and zinc along with it, you know.

"There were about 200 single men working around at the Ymer and maybe another 200 in smaller camps not too far away. We had about 14 whiskey joints here, and maybe five hotels, but they never had girls in any of them. Oh, yes, we had 'em, alright, but they were in a house by themselves across the creek. It was real handy for the Yankee Girl boys, maybe about 11, they depended on the mine boys for a living, of course, and when there weren't enough to keep 'em busy,

some moved to another camp somewhere. Then when we had a boom like we did several times, they'd come back. The boys threw a party for Sally when she came back, they liked her real well.

"The miners had to stay in the boarding houses at the mines until Friday night, then they'd come down here to get drunk and son, you know, they wouldn't go back until Monday morning. Sometimes they couldn't make it and sometimes they never got back at all. The boarding house owners up there got mad, the cooks got paid in the number of meals they fed the men, so some closed down. Then the men had to go back and forth from here, but they brought it on themselves. Oh, they always traveled on saddle horses, though sometimes they caught a ride with other fellows in a buggy. A lot of them were fine men, mostly all young. I've lived here almost sixty years and I made a lot of friends among them, but of course they are all dead now, or else moved away. And no young men come to the town to stay any more, they won't stay at the mine boarding houses any more, either. They have cars now, and what men will work around in the mines or woods either, they can drive back and forth to Salmo or somewhere.

"Oh the mines have mostly shut down long ago, maybe twenty years. There was a boom for a while, and four mills were working for a while but they shut down too. One mill works sometimes, the concentrates they turn out go down to Salmo.

"Small mines don't have a chance any more, those big companies, all they are interested in is a million dollars or so, they won't bother with putting in machinery for a few thousand. There is a lot of gold and silver around still, but its so scattered in small deposits that it never will be mined, don't you know."

BIGGEST HOTEL, the Ymer, was owned for many years by Alexander MacDonald. He ran it as "decent place" and made enough money to support him in old age. When hotel was closed for lack of patronage as mines ceased operations, Alec stayed on as sole resident. He recalls:

"We have as much as ten feet or more of snow every year. I had to go up on the roof and keep it shoveled off so it wouldn't crush the whole building. It just got too much for me when I reached 70, so I had to move out. I've never shoveled the snow since and the roof hasn't collapsed. So I did all that work for nothing."

ORNAMENTS lavishly used as capitals on balcony of Ymer Hotel.

"WHISKEY JOINT with rooms upstairs," long time resident of Ymer, Alec MacDonald says of this building. However rooms served legitimate use as lodgings for men spending "cut 'er loose" weekends in town.

DOOR OF OLD TENDOY STORE stands ajar but guarded by prickly thistle.

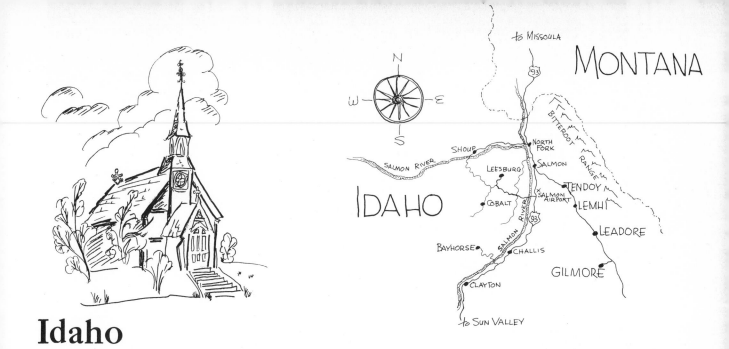

Idaho

NO PLYMOUTH ROCK FOR SEA CAPTAIN JOE

De Lamar, Idaho

Sailing ship skippers who "swallowed the anchor" and quit the sea were said to be fond of settling down to raising Plymouth Rocks instead of keeping ships clear of them. But Joseph R. De Lamar was one sea captain with a mind for mines.

The camp he built up and named for himself was compressed by Idaho's Owyhee Mountains into a narrow gulch and settled by prospectors on the track of nuggets from the "lost" Blue Bucket Mine. The tales of that 1845 incident of children in the Meek overland party finding nuggets in a stream and carrying them along in a blue bucket which disappeared into legend, spread over the West for a time and then died down. Fifteen years later they sprang up again, fortune seekers still hopeful, perhaps of finding the chunk of gold which was said to serve somewhere as a doorstop.

Some searching parties did find rich gold deposits as in Canyon City, Oregon, and these spurred on others. Rumors of rich finds in the comparatively remote Boise Basin of Idaho sparked prospectors

WITHIN SIGHT of old Tendoy store are several log cabins in various stages of decay. This one, long unoccupied, is still in fair condition. Narrow valley where Tendoy is situated lies enclosed by parallel Beaverhead and Lemhi Ranges. Beaverhead forms Continental Divide and at this point boundary between Idaho and Montana. Lesser Lemhi Range seen here in background exhibits characteristic lack of verdure on east-facing slope, most rainfall being trapped on side catching ocean-born moisture. Famed Salmon River flows on other side of Lemhi.

to take loosely organized parties into the Owyhees. One fanciful story combined the Blue Bucket tale with one of nuggets found in an Owyhee stream and Michael Jordan of Placerville pulled together a group to go look for more. In 1863 the men crossed the spring-swollen Snake River, got over the divide and down to a stream later called the Jordan.

Although intending to camp here overnight several of the more impatient removed only the gold pans from the pack horses and got to work in the gravel at once. In an account later written by member O. H. Purdy, Dr. Rudd "had about a hundred colors" in the dregs of his first panning. "The men were jubilant and excited. They ran from one to another exhibiting their discoveries."

This news spread quickly, sending an estimated 2500 men to the Owyhees. That first camp on the Jordan, called Booneville and later Dewey, was soon surrounded by Silver City, Ruby, De Lamar and others (see *Western Ghost Towns*). Although placer gold was quickly exhausted, tremendous deposits of silver kept up the flow of wealth and activity.

The camp of Wagontown was a stopping place on the stage line between Silver City and Jordan Valley, Oregon, and above it were numerous mines and claims. Here in 1888 appeared Capt. Joseph R. De Lamar who bought scattered properties to form one large mining district named for himself. He immediately expanded the cooperating mines, activated dormant claims and set about developing a town in the narrow Jordan Canyon. De Lamar necessarily grew up as a "string town," two rows of buildings wide, about two miles long.

Having spent some $10,000 for his Wilson and adjacent mines, Capt. De Lamar poured an equal fortune into the building of a mill, large hotel, stores and other town essentials, including red light houses at the lower end, almost joining with the original Wagontown. Naturally called Toughtown, there was nothing shoddy about its facilities, the captain providing the best to attract top talent girls from Hailey, an older town going down hill. One of the madames so lured was Jeannie Mitchel and an oldtimer now living in nearby Jordan Valley, Oregon, fondly recollects, "Jeannie's was the best house they ever had in Toughtown."

Jordan Creek, running the length of De Lamar, was a sparkling clear mountain stream before mining in the Owyhees. Then loaded with mill and outhouse wastes in running through Silver City, it became an open sewer when reaching De Lamar. And there, with a long line of outdoor toilets suspended above the creek, it was something more than turbid.

In 1891 De Lamar's newspaper, the *Nugget* reprinted a news item from Chicago stating that a man from Idaho had deposited a check for $463,000 in a La Salle Street bank, the check accepted without question. The local paper added the comment, "As neither of the editors of this paper has been

LEADORE was early center for mining operations in Lemhi Valley and source of supplies for remotely situated farmers and ranchers. Section pictured was center of town. Small false-fronted structure in center advertising its goods and services, one item remaining legible—"Farmers Telephone Exchange."
Leadore once made national headlines when stagecoach was held up on Gilmore Divide just south of town. Road agents took $37,000, barricaded themselves in cliffs above Hahn's Smelter. Infuriated miners who shipped gold stolen smoked bandits out and killed them. Loot was never located, is presumed still hidden in rocky fastness.

DE LAMAR SCHOOL is imposing even now. Second floor was reached by outside stairways, one at each end. At left in rear are seen pair of privies so situated as to drop wastes directly into Jordan Creek.

in Chicago recently and Captain De Lamar has, our readers may readily guess who deposited the check."

Unquestionably the captain was doing well financially. At a time when his mines were producing half a million dollars worth of bullion a month he sold out to an English company for $1,700,000. And to prove his shrewdness the mines then began a slow decline in production that lasted until final closure. It was estimated the total delivery of silver during the life of the mines in De Lamar was at least $8 million.

FEED TROUGHS in old livery stable handily supplied through chute from loft above.

DE LAMAR'S LIVERY STABLE looks comparatively modern with corrugated metal front but actually dates back to days of ox team transportation. At least three ox teams were sheltered here between trips to Silver City and Jordan Valley. Shown above front door are remains of block-and-tackle rig used to hoist hay into loft. Jordan Creek runs directly behind building.

MINER'S CABIN beside road in De Lamar was occupied by lone oldtimer until recent years. Hillsides are too arid to support such moisture-loving trees as cottonwoods, these able to reach water level of creek just across road.

GILMORE STREET parallel on south to one passing meat market leading directly down to Jaggers Hotel just out of photo at left. Visible at right is old gas pump where Peter Amonson hoped to replenish near-empty tank. Cloud shadows darken valley beyond.

DOWN, GILMORE, DOWN

Gilmore, Idaho

The first time Peter Amonson, now of Portland, Oregon, saw Gilmore he was 5 and his small hand was held securely in the big protecting one of his father. The mining camp was roaring then, a hell-and-damnation spot on a flat below the high-perched lead and silver mine which had been producing since 1889. The last time Peter saw the camp it had long departed this earth but there was still violence there. He was slugged with a pistol butt.

When grandfather Peter Amonson came to America from Norway he was all for digging up some of the tons of gold reputedly being easily garnered in Leesburg, Idaho. The town then, in 1865, was the largest gold camp in the state (see *Ghost Town Album*). Amonson saw all the good sites were occupied and was further disillusioned by food prices. "Well," the storekeeper said, "everybody wants to dig gold and there ain't nobody to haul supplies up here."

In a few weeks there was. Amonson outfitted a pack train, was hauling goods and provisions up the steep mountain trail from the Salmon River, provisions like cured meat and eggs which brought a dollar each.

As mining at Leesburg passed into the big-time dredging stage Amonson quit the hauling business and bought a spread of land between Leadore and Lemhi in the valley of the Lemhi River flowing into the Salmon. Son Oscar was born into this ranch life and lived here the length of his days, his son Peter born on the same farm.

The nearby town of Lemhi was settled by colonizing Mormons in 1855 and named for a character in the Book of Mormon. The early farmers did some small scale irrigating and were generally successful. Indians were at first friendly but as the Mormon population increased they realized their lands would eventually all be taken over and retaliated with frequent attacks on the settlement in which some settlers were killed. The Saints were ready to give up when a pronouncement came from Brigham Young that the United States was about to attack Salt Lake City and all brethren in outlying communities were to abandon their homes and return at once to Utah.

Later settlers were friendly with the ruling chief Tendoy (see *Boot Hill*). When he died there was a general Indian exodus which left the villages of Lemhi and nearby Tendoy exclusively to the whites.

In 1940 the teacher in the small Lemhi school was an attractive twenty-one year old, blonde Jean Simonson, and the following year she and cowboy Peter Amonson were married. About six months after the wedding the couple took a delayed honeymoon trip up the Lemhi Valley to see what was left of Gilmore and if any of their old family friends were there. At a point near the short spur leading

JAGGERS HOTEL without paying guests for at least 30 years, is still in fairly good condition. Shown at left is "temporary" entrance where Peter Amonson was pistol whipped.

to the former camp Peter realized the car was nearly out of gas. Could they make it as far as Gilmore and would the old gas pump he remembered still be in service?

They got there safely, found the town nearly deserted and parked near the gas pump in front of an empty store. Amonson found out from an Indian friend that the pump still dispensed gas, the man operating the "station" being the deputy sheriff who lived in a room on the upper floor of the otherwise abandoned hotel across the street.

Getting no response at the main front entry, Amonson and Indian friend went around to the side and pounded on another door. It was finally yanked open by a man obviously drunk. Scowling and staggering, he pulled out a gun and mumbled, "What the hell do you want?" When Amonson asked if he could get some gas, the gun descended on his head and the door was slammed shut. The Indian helped Amonson find his glasses which had flown into the high grass and commented, "I don't believe he wants to sell you any gas." The Amonsons, coasting most of the way, returned home, crossing Gilmore off their list of places to go.

Gilmore's activity started with the organization of the Texas District named for Texas Creek flowing through the gulch. Six years were spent in attempts to get the operation going, to mill the ore locally. Then the Viola smelter was established at Nicholia and William Kesl was awarded the contract to haul the ore with a string of heavy freight wagons and mule teams. Prosperity reigned until the smelter burned when all Texas Creek operations at Gilmore closed down.

In 1902 the mines were purchased by the Pittsburg Company and attempts made to haul ore to Dubois at rail head. Worn out wagons broke down under the heavy loads on rough roads and with replacements being impractical the company tried a steam tractor outfit. This too broke down and in 1907 the mines closed once more. Three years went by in idleness until the Gilmore and Pittsburg Railway was completed with a large roundhouse at Gilmore. Then all signals were "go" with ore now being easily shipped to Armstead, Montana, where it could be forwarded to large smelters. Production in the last year before the depression beginning in 1929 was $11,520,852, this primarily from the Pittsburg-Idaho mine. All major mines closed down early in the '30s, small ones continuing for a time. The death of the mines meant the end of the railroad and the tracks were torn out for salvage.

BUSY STREET in Gilmore passed many business places, drink emporiums. Prominent at right is meat market with sign still faintly legible. On intersecting street below is Jaggers Hotel.

MAIN ENTRANCE of Jaggers Hotel. "Jaggers Annex" at right sported elaborate bar, gambling equipment on main floor, rooms upstairs. Entrance to annex was through vestibule serving in winter as "air lock" against sub-zero blasts.

TWIN TOWNS IN TORMENT

Custer and Bonanza, Idaho

Nobody cared who she was or where she came from as long as she was free and easy and kept her luxurious head of auburn hair, symbol of light and life in Bonanza. And that hair was about all she did keep on her downhill skid to the last ditch. Call her Amanda and if you don't have money just show her a bottle.

❋ ❋ ❋

Trappers searching for pelts along the Yankee Fork of the Salmon River often saw gold gleaming in the creek sands. But they were fur hunters and merely reported matters at the supply settlements on the Salmon. In the spring of 1873 such rumors reached prospector John G. Morrison and set his ears tingling.

He packed into the area described and did find gold but returned to the settlements to hire forty-five men, the entire party being in the gold field before snow fell in the fall. The men immediately began drifting shafts to bedrock, taking advantage of the frozen ground that helped keep earthen walls from collapsing. The tools they had were fine for mining but not for building cabins, so in primitive brush shelters at an elevation of well over 6,000 feet, Morrison's men endured a winter in heavy snows and temperatures probably down to 30 below.

The next summer's operations were profitable and other prospectors swarmed in, some finding little gold, more going away disappointed. The next year William Norton from Michigan made a rich strike but it seemed to be limited to the immediate locality. He removed considerable good ore but had no mechanical way of getting the gold out of it since the area was available only by pack horse. He selected the best of it and in a crude mortar crushed it with a homemade pestle, washing the dust in a conventional pan.

At work one day Morrison was accosted by prospector John Rohrer and over a cup of coffee the two became partners, a safety arrangement in a primitive wilderness where an injured man could die alone. Now one man would dig and select the ore while the other pounded and panned it, the pair recovering in one thirteen-day period $11,000.

The year of truth for the Yankee Fork was 1876 when in August a party of three—James Baxter, E. K. Dodge and Morton McKeim—found some good float not far from where Morrison and Rohrer

were working. Content with what he had, Morrison indicated a ledge as being the likely source of the newcomers' samples and there on the 17th was found the mother lode of Yankee Fork.

In that year it was logical the discoverers name the location Custer Mountain and their workings the General Custer Mine. They set up a simple arrastra, crushed some ore and even this crude operation revealed riches to stagger the three men. They realized they had something that would require development far beyond their financial limits and agreed the best course was to sell out to the English-based firm of Hagan and Grayson. Sale price was not released but a much smaller discovery made the same year was sold to this company for $20,000.

By the summer of 1878 the town of Bonanza was started by Charles Franklin (see *Tales the*

SIDE STREET in Gilmore slopes steeply down to residential section. View looks east over valley of south-flowing Birch Creek at point just south of divide from north-flowing Lemhi River, north of scene of Birch Creek Massacre (see Boot Hill). Black cloud here produces dark shadow on foothills in middle distance. Mountains in background are of Bitterroot Range, here forming Continental Divide and boundary between Idaho and Montana. On other side lie Bannack, Virginia City, other famous early mining camps.

WEATHERED SOUTH SIDE of railroad shack at Gimlet siding offers study in textures.

Western Tombstones Tell), reputed to hail from Bodie, California. With Morrison and other early settlers, Franklin selected the townsite at a point near where Jordan Creek joined Yankee Fork and platted the township, measuring out lots to sell from $40 to $300.

Among the first crude log structures was a large one intended to be a saloon. With walls up and roof of shakes it was warmed by a big dance, re-markable in that the camp had no women. Yet one man who had experience in other camps was equal to the occasion. The men were divided in halves, each on one side having a red bandana tied around his arm to make him a pro tem woman. Any deficiencies caused by such man-to-man com-bat on the dance floor were overcome after a few snorts of stingo from the bar. With music from

INSIDE WALLS of old railroad buildings at Gimlet are decorated with "art" clipped from mail order catalogs, magazines.

ABANDONED STATION identifies location of once busy siding. Grassy tracks, rusty rails attest to infrequency of traffic now. Modern highway to Sun Valley, summit of Sawtooth Mountains and head of Salmon River Valley, passes in left background.

banjo and harmonica, Bonanza's first dance lasted till dawn with little mining or building done the next day.

But ere long, the camp did have a woman. When she arrived in 1879 the men had little curiosity about her other than to ask her name and she told them simply, Amanda. But later arrivals learned she was born in Council Bluffs, Iowa, was educated in a convent school up to the age of 8 then very quickly began learning the facts of life.

The turbulent years of gold and silver strikes in the Sawtooth Mountains saw Amanda working in a bordello in Vienna. A tendency to shack up with one or the other of her favorite customers cost her the job and she moved to Sawtooth City only to have this happen again. She was welcomed in Bonanza, then called Bonanza City, and settled herself in a small cabin at the lower edge of town where she carried on a brisk trade.

She proved to have some knowledge of medicine and nursing and in this camp without doctor or hospital she made herself a soiled angel of mercy. A sick or injured miner might suddenly find Amanda spooning out calomel or scrubbing out his cabin. If a prospector or trapper lay ill in some mountain shack Amanda went to him on her horse, medicine bags tied to her saddle, and staying until the man recovered and longer if both were willing and able.

Added to men, Amanda had a weakness for the bottle. She began going on benders that would last for days and in a few years she was spending the night with any man who asked her, and not often being paid for it. One of her most constant friends now was prospector John Bee who had a cabin on the creek bank.

John was a familiar figure in his favorite saloon where he drank and played poker late into the night. More and more often Amanda would be with him, drinking with him and then sleeping by him on her arm. When he lost all his money one night to another prospector, known ambigu-

SMALL CABIN in good condition owes preservation to cedar boards on roof being almost indestructible.

ORIGINAL BUILDING at Bonanza, built of logs as were most others there, shows excellent craftsmanship, careful fitting of corners. Note marks of broadaxe used in hewing and flattening sides of logs. Chinks were filled with clay and moss, sometimes mixed together. Wooden sidewalks were installed when sawmills appeared. On shelf behind cabins is Bonanza City Branch of U.S. Forest Service, only human habitation in once thriving town. Nearby was large C.C.C. camp in 1935.

ously as Pete, he put Amanda up on what he thought was an unbeatable hand. But Pete showed a better one, bought a bottle of whiskey, toted the sleeping girl to his own cabin.

It was just across the creek from John Bee's and all the next day that worthy moaned and mooned and eyed Pete's cabin. In the morning John crossed the creek, loaded the still sleeping Amanda in Pete's wheelbarrow and trundled her home. He left her only to get a bucket of water but Pete was waiting. He had followed the wheelbarrow tracks and caught Pete with a rifle bullet which struck the boulder he dodged behind. When the second came closer he surrendered—both himself and the girl. So Amanda had her second wheelbarrow ride that day.

In the following years Amanda drifted from one camp to another, moving in all directions including downward. She reached the bottom at Challis

where she was admitted to the Custer County Poorhouse infirmary. When she died at about 60 she appeared as an old woman in every way except for her still luxurious reddish brown hair. Amanda, whose surname was never discovered, was buried in an unmarked pauper's grave at Challis.

Bonanza lay south of the General Custer mine and when the huge mill of the same name was built a short distance north, it made necessary another business and residence center which became Custer. By this time several sawmills were operating and new buildings could be built of lumber. As the population of the new town increased the post office was moved there.

The building program included a road to the outside, actually a trail wide enough to allow passage of wagons pulled by ox teams. The route wound over the high mountains to Challis, the grades so steep heavily loaded wagons were often

LONG ABANDONED RESIDENCE was elaborate for Bonanza where most were single room cabins, original structure enlarged later with lumber. Privy near extreme right, technically "outdoor facility," could be entered from house in winter. View shows two trees most frequently found in area—pines in foreground, junipers scattered on knoll.

snubbed down with ropes looped around trees. It took teamsters five days to make the thirty-five miles and they paid a toll of five cents per pound of freight. All heavy mining and milling machinery had to be hauled in, adding much to an already expensive operation.

In these days most travelers rode horseback and when stages were put into service they, with teamsters, drivers, stage passengers had plenty of opportunity to drink, eat and sleep at numerous way stations. One hostelry, called Homestead Station, was located just below Mill Creek Summit, 9324 feet in elevation. Then there were Toll Gate, Slab Barn and Eleven Mile Barn. One enterprising young lady named Fanny Clark had accommodations in a deep hollow and it was called Fanny's Hole. Later she opened another higher up the mountain and this was christened Fanny's Upper Hole.

The toll road made great changes in Bonanza and Custer. Married women joined their husbands and curtains went up on the windows. Doctors, lawyers and other professional men came in. In her definitive book *Land of the Yankee Fork* Esther Yarber points up many of the characters living there. One was French Godfrey Poquette De Lavallie who was obsessed with plans for the invention of a machine that once set in motion would run forever by its own centrifugal force. He spent most of his life building such gadgets as a large wheel with pockets into which he dropped lead castings of varied weights. When the wheel stopped turning he would sigh and try again. He lived to an old age still trying to perfect his perpetual motion machine.

Early camp life called for talent and ingenuity and one who displayed them dramatically was Col. James McFadden, blacksmith. Finding himself toothless and unable to eat bear steak, so plentiful in the area, he made himself a set of "choppers" said to be as efficient as ones a dentist would turn out. He made the impressions in soft

FIRST BUILDING constructed in Bonanza after sawmill made lumber available.

LONG DEFUNCT GARAGE, originally store building, is well constructed of squared logs.

native clay and eventually hammered out a set of steel teeth complete with a hinge.

While major mine properties were controlled by the English concern all gold produced was shipped to England via railhead at Blackfoot. Shipments were moderate until the General Custer mill opened when large amounts of gold bullion with lesser amounts of silver went by Wells Fargo, one parcel valued at well over $1 million.

By 1890 the twin cities became one, virtually operated by common officials. One business between the two was the small dairy, the cows almost curiosities. Milk was hauled in a large can on a hand cart, the farmer making his rounds of households, dipping out a quart to anybody responding to his bell with a lard bucket.

Before the turn of the century mines in Yankee Fork and other areas had passed into local or at least U.S. ownership. Towns had been through a depression caused by a slump in quality and quan-

tity of ores, and a second boom when rich material was again found. But in 1903 miners generally admitted the end was in sight. There was plenty of gold still in the mountain, they said, but it would take a fortune to drill the tunnels and shafts to reach it. In 1905 extensive plans for such rejuvenation were made in hopes financing would somehow be found and while diligent promoters were scouring the East for money, the Yankee Fork people lived in some sort of suspended vacuum. At first only the easily discouraged moved away but almost all the others, with nothing to live on, were eventually forced to leave.

By 1910 the population was down to a dozen diehards, one family that of Arthur Leslie McGown whose Deardon and McGown store supplied several mines still being worked. The old pioneer hotel, Nevada House, took in an occasional guest until there were none—and no life in the old carcass.

$150,000 DREDGE—When tests in 1937 showed $11 million in gold could be obtained from bed of Yankee Fork, Silas Mason Co. bought rights to dredge gravels. Parts were trucked in and dredge assembled at place of operation, construction finished two years later. Bucket line had 72 units of 8 cu. ft. capacity each.

Operation was more or less continuous until 1952 except when closed down by government with other gold mining operations and occasional severe winter freeze ups. Fully evident in photo is destruction of natural beauty and cover in sportsman's paradise. With merest possibility of rise in gold prices controversy is already raging between dredge owners and conservation forces about voracious monster going back to work.

CUSTER GRADE SCHOOL was second in town and as long as it served was called "new." Built in 1900 it had steeply sloping 4-sided roof to shed heavy snows. Early student was Arthur "Tuff" McGown, enrolled in 1902. He was born in Challis on Salmon River in 1896, moving to Custer as infant. Spending most of his life in Custer, Tuff and wife Edna now operate free museum in old school building, are only residents of one-time boom mining town.

HOME OF PARDEE MINER—Cabin built in typical Montana style, logs spaced for wide chinks of prevailing white clay. Small dam in front yard backed up enough water for this and many other shanties stringing up gulch.

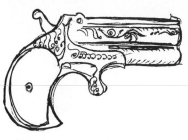

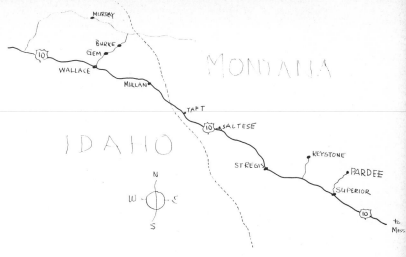

Montana

SILVER VERSUS SAFETY

Pardee, Montana

The vein of silver at Pardee was right on top of the ground. There was a rather good deposit of galena throughout but running along the center was a six-foot wide seam very rich in silver. So said the *Weekly Missoulian* of January 1899 in describing the strike in the mountains four miles from Superior. Added almost as an afterthought was the stinger, "It is ten miles by pack train to the N.P.R.R."

At first the silver-laden ore was wrapped in rawhide bags and packed out on mules. Rough trails were blazed over the mountains north of the mine and down to the Clark Fork. There the ore was loaded on barges and floated down to Paradise, the nearest railroad station, and then to smelters.

During the first several years the mine was operated by the Iron Mountain Mining Co. All ore took the slow, expensive route to refinery and large amounts of profit from sales of concentrates went into improving roads and bridges. Finally the situation was greatly improved by the building of a large mill at the bottom of the final steep grade up to the mine on Flat Creek, with only concentrates to be hauled instead of bulky ore. The mill was soon paid for and during the next several years the complex paid investors half a million dollars.

SUBSTANTIAL LOG BUILDING was hotel for travelers to Pardee. White-flowering shrubs are Philadelphus, state flower of neighboring Idaho.

As time and progress continued the Northern Pacific extended a spur all the way to Superior. The Iron Mountain Co. then built a new mill at railhead with a direct connection to the mines by aerial tramway. In 1906 the company had about 125 on the payroll. At the height of mine and mill prosperity disaster struck through a technicality. The State of Montana passed a law requiring all mines to have two openings as a safety measure. For some unexplained reason Iron Mountain failed to comply with the regulation and was abruptly closed down when the laxity was discovered.

During the next several years there were several attempts to operate the mines but most interested operators agreed that even if the state had not closed down the mine, increasing costs of lifting ore from the depths reached over the years would

have eventually done so. To get around the problem the Iron Mountain Tunnel Co. was organized and plans laid to bore a tunnel horizontally from the bottom of the hill to the 1,600-foot level of the mine. Stock was being sold about 1910 and a year or two later the men promoting the venture leased several hundred acres of ground adjoining.

Apparently no tunnel was ever constructed though some small-scale gophering continued off and on until 1930 when the town was abandoned. Several individual operators were conducting drilling tests on the property as late as 1958. A visit in 1965 uncovered no traces of recent human activity. A Forest Service sign at the foot of the grade up the old rutted, rocky road to the mine read, "Flat Creek Trail. Next 6 miles steep and narrow with switchbacks."

SHODDY STRUCTURES of Pardee's unsavory section built on narrow bench of level ground above Flat Creek including saloons, gambling houses, prostitutes' cribs. Some buildings have completely collapsed, others totter. All faced sparkling creek that divided disrepute and respectability.

NOTES ON A GOLD PAN

Gold Creek, Montana

The diaries of early miners who were perhaps conscious of the parts they were playing in history "oft remind us . . . footsteps in the sands of time"—and forsooth, in the sands of creek beds. Panning the gold in the diaries of Gold Creek miners turns up some interesting color.

In 1862 the camp was a place where a man could go unshaven, let his hair grow to his shoulders and remain unwashed for weeks, particularly in winter. When his clothing bothered even him, he might wash it, but why hurry? All this was before women and when one or two did appear in camp, he changed his tune—and clothes.

An item in Granville Stuart's diary on July 12, 1862, covers the point. "With the emigrants today is Mr. B. Burchet with his family. . . . Miss Burchet is sixteen years old and a very beautiful girl. Every man in camp has changed and changed his shirt since the family arrived. We are all trying to appear like civilized men."

And on July 23: "Arrived in town today a fine violin player accompanied by his handsome seventeen year old wife. . . . All the men are shaving nowadays and most of them indulge in an occasional haircut. The blue flannel shirt with a black tie has taken the place of the elaborately beaded buckskin one. The white men are wearing shoes instead of moccasins and most of us have selected some other day than Sunday for washday." That same year Granville put an end to his own loneliness by marrying Aubony, a Snake Indian girl whom he described as "a fairly good cook, amiable and with few relatives."

Another Gold Creek miner, James Stuart, brother of Granville and sheriff of Missoula County, recorded in his diary that year, "I brought with me the Indian woman ransomed from Narcisse, the Flathead. She is rather good looking, and seems to be of good disposition. . . . I could do worse, so I find myself a married man." And this Stuart had other pursuits besides the good wife, as he wrote later, "I have lost three hundred dollars today, staking a man to deal monte for me the past three days. I think I will take Granville's advice and quit gambling." The next day he observed, "Our monte sharps are about to take the town. Getting decidedly obstreperous in their conduct," he observed sharply.

The next day two men named Fox and Bull arrived from Elk City in the Clearwater Mountains with the word that they were looking for some card sharps that had been run out of their town but not before they could ride away on horses belonging to prominent citizens. One of the two-man posse carried a double-barreled shotgun heavily loaded with buckshot, the other a Colt navy revolver.

Sheriff James Stuart told them the wanted men might be in Worden and Co.'s store where one of them, Spillman, went to buy a shirt. With the shotgun aimed at his heart Spillman meekly surrendered, Fox and Bull delegating a guard to hold

GOLD CREEK, once so full of violence, is today a mere huddle of ramshackle buildings. Boards and battens conceal original log construction of many relics. Photo depicts crossroads center of town where monte dealer Arnett was gunned down with cards in one hand, gun in other.

him while the sheriff led them to a saloon where the other card sharp and horse thieves Arnett and Jermagin were just about to open a new monte game.

Though dealing, Arnett had his loaded revolver handy in his lap. At the command of "hands up" he reached for the weapon but had no time to raise it, taking a charge of buckshot through the breast. Jermagin ran to the nearest corner crying, "Don't shoot! I give up!" He was quickly tied up and put under guard with Spillman. Arnett died with the monte cards in his left hand, gun in his right, and neither could be wrenched from his grasp after rigor mortis had set in. He was buried with the tools of his trade still close to him.

At a "miners' trial" Spillman testified he and Arnett left Elk City with six horses and found Jermagin walking, so they gave him a horse to ride. Acquitted of horse theft the judge gave Jermagin six hours to leave town. Having little to pack and no stomach for delay, he made it in that many minutes.

In referring to the affair later Stuart wrote, "Spillman, who was a large, fine looking man was found guilty and sentenced to be hanged in a half hour. He made no defense and seemed to take little interest in the proceedings. . . . He walked to his death with a firm step and seemed as little concerned as if he had been a mere spectator instead of the main actor in the tragedy. It was the firmness of a brave man who saw that death was inevitable and nerved himself to meet it."

Gold Creek had a physician who doubled as an "armchair prospector," disdaining the actual digging and panning in the sand and mud. Granville Stuart wrote, "Doctor Atkinson is a most original character. He is always traveling about the country with a pack and horse and one or more companions. . . . He rides up a canyon keeping on the ridge where possible. From some point of vantage he takes out his field glasses and scours the country visible. Then he declares 'I think that section looks good.' Sometimes he will buy a claim and resell it. On the whole he does as well as most of us who dig innumerable holes and pan innumerable pans of gravel, only succeeding in just missing the streak of pay dirt."

Brothers James and Granville Stuart were in Gold Creek after trouble in Yreka, California. Suffering near starvation, encounters with hostile Indians and disappointing results in claims, they moved north to Montana. Wildly optimistic at first, they wrote a third brother, Thomas, in Colorado, to "hurry here before the place is overcrowded." Thomas came but so did hundreds of other hopefuls following the news of gold in the Deer Lodge area. Most of them were disappointed, the deposits at Gold Creek soon showing signs of depletion under the army of shovels. When word of gold discoveries at Bannack, Alder Gulch and Last Chance reached Gold Creek almost everybody was in a mood to travel and in a few weeks the town was virtually abandoned.

The Stuart brothers deserted too when they heard miners at Bannack diggings would turn over their gold for beef after months of stewed rabbit. Thomas, Granville and James drove the cattle they had been accumulating to Grasshopper Creek and spent the winter selling and dealing.

PIONEER DAYS IN PIONEER

Pioneer, Montana

Take pity, Miss Fanny,
    The belle of Pioneer
And grant some indulgence
    To a vendor of beer
Whose heart rending anguish
    Will bring on decline
Oh, God of creation
    I wish you was mine.

The Pioneer bartender who prostrated himself before Fanny and heaven in these blood-letting lines inserted in the *Cedar Creek Pioneer* never got farther into the annals of this gold camp but it is hoped that with all this soul baring he won Fanny's fancy and did not have to turn the muzzles of too many beer mugs on himself.

Lack of female solace was no doubt a problem but the hard workers seem to rise above it. Like W. A. Clark who became a senator and power in Montana, and Mr. Bio on mining company boards. In later years he told how he got his start as a banker in the tiny gold camp of Pioneer. The banker's books were usually carried under his hat, he said, his vaults his buckskin bag of gold dust and a pair of six-shooters. The miner had hazy ideas about the value of gold. With an actual worth of $20 to $25 an ounce, he paid the miner a flat $18 and later sold it at a figure quoted by the Denver mint.

Prospectors who deserted Gold Creek for better pickings went up one creek and down another, pausing in such sparsely settled places as Squaw Gulch, French Gulch, Woods Flat and Wilson Bar. Pioneer was another and it grew to maybe two thousand people.

Henry Thomas was one of the displaced prospectors but not one to wash out a few pans of gravel and then head for the nearest saloon. He sank a shaft to reach bedrock and rigged up a windlass with bucket and sluice boxes. Without lumber or nails the resourceful loner hand-hewed boards from small trees, fastened them together with wooden pegs. The boards used for sluicing were about eight inches wide and seven feet long, necessitating a tremendous amount of labor before he could even begin mining.

Once ready to wash gravel Thomas let the crude bucket down into the hole, slid down the rope, filled the bucket with gravel and climbed out hand over hand, lifting the load by the windlass. Encountering boulders, he trussed them with ropes and used a crude block-and-tackle to get them out. Gravel was washed in the leaky sluice boxes where the riffles caught most of the gold, he hoped. After two seasons of this prodigious labor he found he averaged one dollar a day, never more than a dollar and a half. The same sort of set-up was frequently operated by partners so one man could stay in the hole, but Henry Thomas preferred his own company. Since he never drank or gambled he may have accumulated more gold dust than those who worked and wasted more efficiently.

Pioneer saw its best years in the 1870s, the main

PAT WALL'S DREDGE sits sadly at edge of pond of own making between Gold Creek and Pioneer. Almost any stranger encountered here will be either ghost town buff or ardent fisherman.

street parallel with the creek lined on both sides by cabins and business houses—two hotels, four general stores, blacksmith shops, livery stables, saloons and gambling houses. It was said that in the latter six faro games were kept running simultaneously.

The camp always had a large Chinese population. In 1879 there were 200 Orientals and 500 whites toiling in the gulches. When values began thinning, the latter gradually withdrew and a Chinese contractor named Tim Lee brought in 800 of his countrymen to comb the leavings. They did it the hard way, removing the impeding layer of rocks and carrying it away in baskets. After cleaning the exposed area, the rocks were replaced in order to open new beds. When even this painful process failed to yield a speck or two, the Chinese moved away and Pioneer was a near ghost.

PIONEER BUILDING shattered into rubble. The **Montana Standard** in 1929 predicted what would happen to the old ghost town of Pioneer with advent of Pat Wall's monster dredge. Referring to the several stone structures at lower edge of town, "The old post office will be converted into a bunk house. The bank will be a restaurant, the bank vaults a pantry, for the building of dressed stone is cool enough to keep food fresh without ice." These buildings, spared by dredge operations, stood intact long enough to be sketched by Colorado artist Muriel Wolle and photographed for dust jacket of **Shallow Diggings** by Jean Davis.

Intact in these pictures, the buildings were magnets for this author but in 1965 he found them in ruins. Inquiry of man working for modern concern again digging for gold at Pioneer City, brought explanation, "Our company would have saved the buildings but when money-mad county authorities found we were working here they slammed us with huge taxes for what they called usable buildings, so we deliberately wrecked them."

About 1893 an English firm called Gold Creek Mining Co. Ltd. moved in with a dredge to work the much hand-labored gravels and right away ran into trouble. A few remaining residents resented the big scale removal of gold and obstructed operations by damming the stream above the work field. Rather than force the issue, the company resorted to litigation that dragged on for years.

About 1927 a Butte promoter bought out the English firm which was thoroughly sick of the whole business. The new dredge owner, Pat Wall, now purchased the whole area—town, surrounding land, water rights—acquiring 3,200 acres of hills and gulches. He also bought a monster dredge costing $250,000 and required forty-two freight cars to bring it from California.

A newspaper of the day editorialized, "... with brick and stone and lumber will go apple trees and lilac bushes brought in on the backs of pack animals ... the entire town of Pioneer is about to be fed into the maw of a huge dredge." It almost was. The dredge ran alongside the town which was built on a bench and escaped actual engorgement, but the row of buildings nearest the mine workings was buried in a deep layer of rocky dumps, leaving a single row of now crumbling structures staring at a long ridge of barren rocks.

LOG HOUSE with large roof extension seems unfinished, no marks of usual roofing boards showing. Certainly style would have been practical in country of heavy snowfall, preventing blockage at entrance, usual result of overnight storms (see another view of street with dredge tailings in **Boot Hill**).

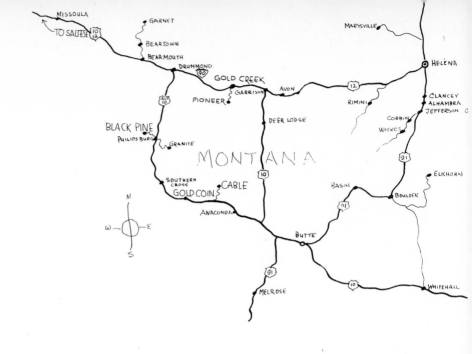

THE LOST HORSE GOLD

Cable, Montana

"The first place of note is a forlorn looking town with two idle quartz mills, many deserted and torn down houses and but one solitary inhabitant. . . . The hillside below the discovery had been washed bare to the bedrock . . . this alone· yielded nearly $100,000." This description from the *Rocky Mountain Husbandman* could well fit many a mining camp as found today but the date on the clipping is September 26, 1878. Gleaned by Muriel Sibell Wolle for her comprehensive book *Montana Pay Dirt* the item shows Cable became a ghost town early. It also points out that ghostly conditions are

not necessarily permanent. Cable sat up from somnolence, living on until 1940.

Many a gold mine was located through cooperation of a horse, burro or cow or even as a slain bird as at Vulture, Arizona. In Cable's case, in the early summer of 1867, prospectors Alexander Aiken, James Stough and John E. Pearson made their camp for the night. Next morning the horses were gone and in tracking them the men came across a bed of decomposed, crumbling quartz. Scattered throughout were bits of shining gold, released in the weathering of the top of what turned out to be a nearly vertical chimney of auriferous quartz extending downward about 1000 feet.

As soon as the horses were located the excited men crushed some of the ore in their hand mortars, carried a few pounds of it down to the creek,

BOARDING HOUSE YARD was first place wide enough for author to turn pickup camper around. Cookhouse shown attached to rear. Several photos were hastily made before leaving old camp of Atlantic Cable.

nearly a mile away. They panned it out and calculated they might well make $30 a day per man.

Later when machinery was installed values showed $18 per ton but rich pockets frequently encountered ran it up to between $100 and $1,000. Even so, news of the strike at Cable did not immediately attract the usual influx of prospectors due to the scanty population of Montana spread thinly among other camps.

The three partners had trouble making wages because of the distance to water necessary for sluicing so they agreed to stop panning long enough to build a conduit, part flume, part ditch, and the four-mile waterway was completed by fall.

As soon as snow began to melt in the spring the trio was able to sluice out enough gold for capital to enlarge operations.

The discoverers took the precaution of immediately staking out not only the original claims but five additional 200-foot ones above and five below. Convinced they had something going they delegated one man to go to Deer Lodge, 35 miles away, and record everything in legal fashion, the name selected Atlantic Cable Lode, commemorating the successful laying of the second trans-ocean cable.

The painfully constructed sluiceway proved inadequate for increasingly large operations. With more capital from Helena bankers, a 20-stamp mill

GOLD COIN MINE was one of complex below and around Cable which included Southern Cross, Pyrenees, Stuart, Hidden Lake, Red Lion etc. Old maps showing mine, mill and camp locations give impression they were crowded together. Actual access was hindered by ravines, mountains, gulches. Travel time from one camp to neighbor might be hours or days. Shown here is famous old Gold Coin mill, still fairly well preserved. Ore was handled by gravity system, reason so many mills were built on steep hillsides. Mine dumps shown at extreme right, trestle that carried ore cars to big door at upper end of mill. Rough chunks of material dumped at top of incline fell by stages thru grinding, pulverizing, chemical processes to emerge as concentrates at bottom.

RUINS OF OLD BARN beyond which on road to Cable visitor encounters gate posted against entry. Author was forced to continue since there was no turning space at gate.

was erected on the creek at about the point where the first crushed ore was panned out. Success was indifferent as amalgamation methods were not effective on this particular ore. One man said at the time, "Most of the gold is going down the creek." Even so, with selection of only the richest ore for processing, the mill turned out $30,000 the first year.

Banker William Nowlan thought well enough of results to buy into the claim. According to one authority Alexander Aiken, one of the three original discoverers, did not agree with the new policies and after several furious arguments, instituted suit against the firm. Succeeding legal hassles wiped

out his entire fortune and Aiken left the country on foot, all his belongings in a pack.

Through the 1870s one misfortune after another came to Cable. Good paying leads were lost because of crude, awkward mining methods. With an almost complete lack of ore the main mill was forced to close and then banker Nowlan died, intensifying litigation that had never entirely ceased. Doubt and uncertainty so undermined confidence of other backers they withdrew and things at Cable came to a standstill in 1877.

In that year J. C. Slavery, brother-in-law of Nowlan, began proceedings to straighten out the mess and in some two years acquired clear title to

Atlantic Cable. In 1883 he ran a long tunnel from the hillside in hopes of contacting the vein at a lower level. He felt so sure of doing this that while work on the tunnel was going on he erected a 30-ton mill costing $65,000. Slavery must have been born under a different star than his predecessor for about the time the mill was finished a rich pocket of gold was struck that paid his $150,000 expense within thirty days.

Being a trusting soul he put a man named Jewell in charge as foreman and paid no further attention to details of managing the miners. In time he heard rumors that some of his men were displaying untoward signs of affluence, considering their daily wage of $3. Several had built fancy homes and bought farms down the valley. Many of them were "Cousin Jacks" and Slavery learned of relatives back in Cornwall naming a street Cable Terrace to commemorate the mine that made it possible for so many emigrants to buy fine homes in America. When he did launch an investigation he found some $60,000 in gold nuggets had been "high-graded" in 1883 alone. He then put in effect a rule requiring all workmen to strip for examination when passing out the gate at the end of their shifts.

The Cable produced a fortune in the next few years, then the output began a varied performance that rose and fell until Slavery closed the property in 1891. Total production until then was about $3,500,000. Eventually the workings came to life again in the salvage of ores wasted in previous crude methods. After 1906, brothers H. C. and F. W. Bacon did some development work, running three shifts a day, but these operations ceased in 1940 and Cable again became a ghost town. The properties are now posted against visitors because of vandalism, the present owners very likely hoping gold values will eventually increase enough to warrant reopening.

FRONT ENTRANCE to Cable's old boarding house. Board and batten construction was usual in area lacking proper stone.

OLD OPHIR CEMETERY about ½ mile above town, cradled in circle of spectacular San Juan peaks, Uncompahgres. Background peaks here reach over 14,000'. Scant forest cover alternates between light-colored aspens barely leafing out and dark evergreens, alpine firs, spruces. Blue Colorado sky vaults above carpet of solid gold dandelion blooms between graves.

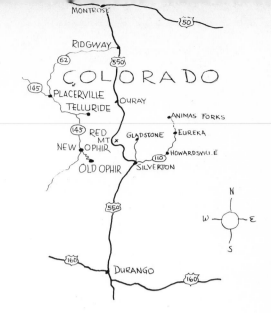

Colorado

SO RICH IN GOLD

Ophir, Colorado

The first party to explore for mineral veins at the foot of Ophir Needles was a group led by Lt. Howard who founded Howardsville near Silverton. He tarried in Colorado long enough to bestow his name once more, on a stream tumbling down the valley, a branch of the San Miguel River, he called Howard's Fork.

The first legal claims were staked there in 1875 and from then on prospectors dribbled through and sometimes stopped for a while. Nobody stayed all winter at this near-timberline elevation until 1878-9 when seventeen men did hole up there, working their claims whenever weather allowed, which was seldom. Some burrowed under banks of deep snow for some protection from frigid blasts off the 14,000-foot peaks.

The next year the Osceola mine was producing some gold and from others like the Gold King came sack after sack of rich ore. One batch of ten brought the owners $5,000. These miners were able to use arrastras which, though crude, were effective when ore was rich enough. One enthusiastic Howard's Fork miner suggested renaming the place Ophir after the fabled Arabian city so rich in gold.

About the time five hundred prospectors were swarming around Ophir, working up thirsts that required five saloons to put down, carbonate fever struck. At Leadville where gold was growing scarce, miners discovered the heavy rocks they cursed as obstacles to gold mining were loaded with carbonate of lead, and with lead inevitably came silver. This inspired many second thoughts about areas where other gold placers were exhausted, one of these being Rico, erstwhile heavy gold producer. Sure enough, the place was now found to be "rico" in silver. Since it was near Ophir its miners were caught up in the prevailing excitement and left the camp almost deserted, a ghost town before it was fairly alive.

Where Leadville's carbonate deposits were so extensive as to create the greatest boom of its kind, those at Rico were disappointingly small and soon exhausted. So the tide turned and Ophir miners rushed back to their old claims. With the building

THRU THIS PORTAL passed some of Colorado's ugliest men. Most early mining camps had a few denizens who were fugitives from eastern law.

OLD OPHIR JAIL, only building standing in central part of business district which had famous Colorado House, other hotels, stores, saloons, gambling houses. More solidly built for security, jail's heavy logs and beams have resisted gales, snows of nearly century. Town had good water supply, fire protection (note hydrant, right).

In middle distance of photo are scattered remains of business houses, now mercifully graced with blanket of brilliant yellow dandelions. Just right of center in far distance is steep trail to summit of pass up which route many tons of gold rich ore was carried on backs of burros to Silverton before railroad. First mail came in this route. At base of last switchback, mail carrier Swen Nilson was buried in snow slide, body not exposed for two years (see **Tales the Western Tombstones Tell**).

of smelters at Silverton, Ophir miners sent their ore by burro trains over and through the mountains to the city at the foot of Sultan Mountain (see *Tales the Western Tombstones Tell* and *Western Ghost Towns*).

In the summer of 1879 "official" mail service from Silverton was established. Muriel Sibell Wolle relates that the service, though welcome, left something to be desired and cites some items from the Ouray *Times* which had a correspondent at Ophir. "The mail carrier from Silverton . . . has robbed the mail and left the country. The mail bag cut open and with registered mail rifled has been found near Iron Springs." Another item: "No mail for weeks. The Kansas tenderfoot says he wouldn't carry the mail again for $5,000 after one trip." And—"No mail from Rico in ten days. The snow is nearly ten feet deep and there are snow slides in every gulch . . . the mail carrier nearly froze on his last trip."

REMAINING RESIDENCES, only buildings at Old Ophir, these in far better condition than those in New Ophir which was little more than station on highway from which two cars of Ophir mine ore were shipped daily. These houses were occupied until recently. Porches, decorations such as barge-boards have been added in later years, old photo from Fred and Jo Mazula collection in **An Empire of Silver** showing them without porches, etc.

HOME OF THE FAMOUS SMUGGLER

Telluride, Colorado

The Union and Sherman mines were good producers of silver and other metals in 1876 and in July of that year prospector J. B. Ingram grew curious about them. They seemed farther apart on the mountainside than they should be and sure enough, by measurement he found several hundred feet not legally included in either. So shortly he had a claim, a mine, a fortune.

He named the mine The Smuggler and when it proved to be richer than either of its neighbors, its owner bought out both of them. The name Ingram is perpetuated in a spectacular waterfall dropping many hundreds of feet down a precipitous cliff at the north edge of Telluride.

The name of this old camp was not included in early accounts as it was born when residents of San Miguel wanted to live nearer the mountainside mines, under the towering peaks of the San Juans. And since the ores in the area were mostly telluride, a compound containing tellurium, a non-metallic element analogous to sulphur and selenium, this suggested the word Telluride for the new camp.

The town had its full quota of bad men, those trying to be bad and others trying to keep them subdued, one of its most famous marshals being Jim Clark. Besides carrying the usual number of six-shooters Clark stashed several Winchester rifles in stores strategically located around town. He did not hang around saloons, just glancing in one or the other as he walked his regular beat. And his method worked, Telluride being comparatively peaceful for an isolated mining camp during his rather short regime. The end of it came abruptly one dark night when he was slain by an unknown assailant concealed between two buildings.

Without pasture land, Telluride and other camps in the steep-walled San Juan country, had to import all cattle—often from Texas—as well as hogs, sheep and food staples. The porkers, chickens and sacked goods had to be brought in wagons, at first hauled by ox teams. Hillsides were often far too steep to keep a wagon upright and a teamster would borrow a plow from his load, hitch it behind one of his oxen or mules and run a deep furrow along the up side. Then he might take poles carried for such purposes and place them to extend outwards and uphill. All available men would hang on the ends as the steepest spots were passed with upper wheels in the furrow.

In the draw to the east of Telluride, near Pandora, there was a small meadow generally used to hold livestock intended for slaughter, abattoir conveniently near. Meat and potatoes were essential food with some bacon, eggs and salt pork. Ham brought about 16c a pound, beef 8c. Long winters at high altitudes kept food without refrigeration. Women were scarce but a few sold bread and pies made of dried apples and peaches. Although miners averaged only $3 to $3.50 for a ten or twelve hour day, food prices were correspondingly low. The single men who ate in company boarding houses were well fed since labor was always in short supply.

Census reports, when taken in remote camps like Telluride, always reported male to female proportions. Typical were such listings as 300 men, 5 women—560 men, 20 women. Many men, while willing to visit cribs, longed for wives and the camp's little 4-page newspapers produced on a Washington hand press, always carried several ads by a lonely hearts club. A woman might travel to

TELLURIDE'S ASPECT from the front is much like other fading but still alive old towns. True character of many old structures is revealed at rear. Here no paint or repairs detract from genuine atmosphere of old mining camp.

RED MOUNTAIN with white mantle. **Stampede to Timberline** is a veritable text book for students of Colorado's romantic mining history. Author Muriel Sibell Wolle includes passage that gives meaning to photo, "From the Million Dollar Highway, these mines cover an area of about four miles in length and behind them Red Mountain looms up like a backdrop to some Wagnerian opera with the mines and buildings as the details in the setting." Two-story boarding house, saloons and other buildings once crowding both sides of Red Mountain Town are gone, most destroyed by series of fires. One old timer recalled that when fire broke out in Red Mountain Hotel everybody carried out bedding, pool tables, roulette wheels, formed huge pile in middle of street. Then wind shifted, turning flames on heap, destroying everything. First activity at scenic location was in 1879 and in 1890s "lights never went out, gambling halls never closed."

the high mountain camp to be shocked at first meeting a proposed mate. Robert L. Brown, in his book *An Empire of Silver*, relates how one such lady, on arriving at her destination, was dismayed at the first sight of her intended, a big raw-boned, homely Swede. She was ready to go back on the train but the man's friends assured her he was honest, industrious, and would be a good provider. The mail-order bride changed her mind.

Telluride today is still home for several hundred people who refuse to leave their mountain aerie. One woman told the author, "I came here with my husband who is dead now. I used to live in Leadville. When I was a small girl there my family lived in a nice house just below Fryer Hill where the Matchless Mine was. Mrs. Tabor, the one people call Baby Doe now, lived up there in a little shack. She often came down to the town and when she walked along the streets the children always teased her because she dressed so poorly. In win-

ter she often wrapped up her feet in burlap sacks. One day I went into our kitchen and there she sat beside the stove, having a cup of hot tea. I was scared because I had often hollered at her along with the rest of the kids and was going to turn and run. Mrs. Tabor said to me, 'Don't be frightened, child. Your mother invited me in because I was cold and I'll leave as soon as I've finished my tea.' I stayed and we began to talk. She really was very nice and not at all like the horrible old woman the kids called her. She got to dropping in often and we became good friends. I told my friends about how nice she really was and from then on they never called her names again."

This elderly lady, janitress at the old courthouse, asked that she not be named. She is one of the few remaining who would remember Colorado's big mining days and who could say they talked with Haw Tabor's wife, Baby Doe.

FREQUENT GAPS among Telluride's old buildings were caused by fires often plaguing mountain-bound town. In this vacant lot town fathers gathered up some old time water wagons used in fighting fires with other aging vehicles and relics loved by visitors. Telluride offers many attractions to mining camp buffs but is remote from population centers, accounting for nearly deserted streets. Services like gas stations, etc., are still available.

OURAY is one of those Colorado mining camps now much shrunken from rip-roaring center it once was, yet far from ghost. These historic spots can hardly with any justice be omitted from consideration in a pictorial record. Originally called Uncompahgre City for stupendous mountain range hemming it in, later name honoring Ouray, chief of Western Utes, friend to all whites, miners and settlers.

At time when town was terrified by rumors of advancing savage White River Ute tribes, Ouray and wife Chipeta walked up main street with hands upraised in peace gesture. When apprehensive crowd gathered, dignified chief assured citizens he would guarantee their safety from warring segment.

OLD CABIN at Iola dates from earliest days of settlement. With no lumber as yet available, settlers cut pines in mountains, shaped them into something like squareness with such hand tools as broadaxe and adz. Chinks here are narrow because of accurately fitted ends, are chinked with clay inside.

STREET IN OURAY, early supply center for gold, silver mines scattered at higher elevations. These included Camp Bird, owned by Thomas Walsh. There as at many camps snow covered buildings all winter. With advent of electrical power lights were kept burning around clock.

Only road, U.S. 550, reaching Ouray from north, enters town thru narrow notch on comparatively level grade from Montrose. In otherwise perfect circle stony cliffs rise steeply to heights towering almost directly above old camp. From Ouray "Million Dollar Highway" snakes up precipitous grades along narrow canyons, past Red Mountain and at last down to Silverton.

FORLORN CLUSTER of buildings constituting ghost town of Iola slowly weather into decaying shambles. Never a mining camp, tiny town had store and livery stable, serving outlying camps such as Headlight, Old Lott, Anaconda and mile and a half distant Spencer.

Butte in left background is good example of many hills left when material eroded except where protected by portion of hard rimrock. In near right foreground are green, growing tumbleweeds (Russian thistle) seldom noticed in verdant condition. More familiar dry one from last year is seen lodged against log building in accompanying photo.

DISASTER IN THE COAL CAMP

Crested Butte, Colorado

Black clouds still rolled out of the coal mine shaft and a man crawled out with them. He was burned black, far beyond immediate recognition, and for a time seemed the sole survivor. Yet some others did get out, eleven, more dead than alive. One, able to speak coherently, said he was among a group entering the mine for the day's work. He was knocked down and lay unconscious for a while, then started crawling along the floor where the air seemed better. "I know I crawled over several men that seemed very dead to me."

This was the blast that on January 24, 1884, shook Crested Butte to its very foundations. All buildings around the mouth of the mine were demolished, coal cars shot out of the tunnel, debris scattered more than a hundred feet. The new ventilator fan was the first casualty, making it impossible for rescuers to enter the smoky, fume-filled entrance.

There were several coal mines in production at Crested Butte in the early 1880s but one more than equalled the output of all the others. Tunnels stretched farther, shafts went deeper. A natural result was the accumulation of gas and after many complaints the company installed the giant fan to drive fresh air into the depths. Company officials said, "In case of an explosion, fumes and smoke can be eliminated quickly."

This statement was proved wrong. As the news of the January blast spread, miners from Baldwin and other camps quit work and came to Crested Butte on special trains to aid in rescue work. The first group to get in as far as the first level, 200 feet down, found a collection of seventeen bodies. Although it was impossible to penetrate deeper for more than a moment it was obvious many more dead lay at lower levels.

Gunnison historian Betty Wallace, gleaning her

LITTLE RURAL SCHOOLHOUSE beside road from Gunnison to Crested Butte, one of few remnants of one time stopping place for travelers on way to mines in area. At intersection was home of Jack Howe, giving first name to spot, Howville, then Jack's Cabin. Around center grew two hotels, two grocery stores, two saloons, one post office.
Gone now are roistering freighters who stayed here when conveying supplies to mines, ore and coal back to Gunnison. Gone too are all buildings except one-room school house of 80-odd years ago, ranch children still attending classes until very recently. Lush clumps of yellow dandelions make bright spots of color in yard.

data from newspapers of the day, wrote, "Huddled around the shattered entrance families of the unfortunate men stood in shocked silence ... there was no outcry, but muffled sobbing when—thirty-eight hours after the explosion—the first body was brought to the surface, wrapped in canvas, a card of identification pinned to the breast." The process continued until fifty-nine bodies lay in the blacksmith shop pressed into service as a morgue. Several of the victims were teen-age boys on their first job. Most men were found lying on the ground with handkerchiefs over their mouths, indicating deaths by suffocation rather than concussion by the blast.

Although Crested Butte attained its pinnacle of importance in Colorado for its tremendous production of coal, there were placers on Slate and Coal Creeks and some silver and lead. In *Colorado Gold and Silver Mines* by Frank Fossett, published in 1880, are found some pertinent items. The Crested Butte District included such silver-lead mines as the Poverty Gulch group, Independence, Silver, Spence, Renselaer, Wolverine, Silver Queen and numerous others. Considerable ore was treated in Crested Butte, the book states, "A smelter was erected there in 1879, which will probably be steadily employed hereafter." Fossett was derogatory about the quality of Crested Butte coal. "While the veins of North and South are excellent lignite, those of Gunnison are considered anthracite of very inferior quality to that of Pennsylvania." In later years when quality was ignored, it was conceded that the Crested Butte deposits were the only ones of any extent west of the Pennsylvania fields. Very likely the first coal mined here provided the fuel for the smelter mentioned by Fossett. In 1880 there was a collection of tents at the location and after Howard Smith brought in a sawmill, many workers' homes were built.

Before another year passed coal mining was vastly expanded and herds of cattle were pastured nearby, a town built big enough to support a newspaper, the Crested Butte *Republican,* and to be incorporated as a city. By 1882 the railroad was in and coal shipped out more easily. An ultra-modern station was built near where some two hundred burros were still loaded daily with supplies for remote gold, silver and copper mines in the mountains.

Snow at the 9,000-foot altitude of Crested Butte fell almost continually through the winter and by spring often reached twenty-foot depths. Travelers forced to take routes over the passes were in constant dread of the "White Death," as every spring saw avalanches that usually took lives.

In late February, 1891, Edward Clark, superintendent of the Bullion King mine above Crested Butte, went to the city on important business. Before leaving he stopped at one of the saloons for a warmer-upper and as he headed for the door he asked his cronies, "Boys, if I get caught in a snow slide, will you come up to dig me out?" Arriving back at the mine days later he saw the entire complex of boarding houses and offices had been swept cleanly away in a mile-long avalanche. There was no trace of his house where he had left wife and baby.

Fred Germaine tumbled downhill in the shattered boarding house and later told the story. Starting just under the summit of Ruby Peak where snows were deepest, the slide moved down with a tremendous roar. Picking up the boarding house, superintendent's house, engineer's cabin and engine house, the great white wall carried everything to the bottom of the steep slope. Of the personnel, Germaine alone was alive when dug out four hours after the slide. The bodies were brought into

Crested Butte on sleds that required nine men to pull them, so difficult to traverse were the deep snows. The effort of search and rescue was so exhausting and danger from further slides so great, that when several avalanches occurred in March, no rescue crews were sent out until snows melted.

Crested Butte survived as a coal camp even when smelters ceased to operate, but when locomotives turned to diesel fuel, they gave the kiss of death to the town. Some stores still survive here to serve ranchers and sportsmen.

MAIN STREET of old coal camp displays relics of days when town had large population. Buildings shown here are unoccupied but others at western end of street are now used as stores, museum, antique shops.

PANORAMIC VIEW of Crested Butte shows cemetery in foreground, many graves those of mine explosion, avalanche victims. Funeral services, burials for those men dying in 1884 blast required a week, all flags at half mast. 3' of snow lay on ground frozen so hard grave diggers left cavities shallow. Next spring several small boys exploring cemetery found some caskets protruding from ground, fled home to report gruesome discovery. Hasty reburial followed.

CRESTED BUTTE at confluence of Slate and Coal Creeks is having some revival as ski area, with Gunnison as nearest center of population. In summer small stores amply serve fishermen, hunters. In some areas coal, once mainstay of economy, is being mined, pulverized, jet-sprayed in steam plants generating electricity where water power is scarce, as in Great Basin. This view behind old buildings shows most windows high up, above winter snow line. Outdoor "johns" were two-story affairs for unknown reason. In center of photo is cluster of rabbit hutches, one in every back yard.

PICTURESQUE BUILDING on left built by Jake Kochevar, one of Crested Butte's predominantly Slavic population. He cut fancy shingles on home for jigsaw effect. His son, interviewed by telephone in 1967, says structure was built as residence in spite of commercial look with false front, other decorations, and that another structure across street bearing similar ornaments, was also private residence. Building at right served many years as boarding house, upper floor giving onto front porch, once part of balcony along side.

DETAILED VIEW of facade, Jake Kochevar home. Slavonian took great pride in building, cutting elaborate shingles by hand. In larger population centers this kind of ornamentation was fad around turn of century, fancy-cut shingles being commercially available. In many shingle mills some sorted as to size were tightly packed in bundles, ends cut to desired shape all at once on band saw. Author has noted many examples of once popular craft, none more perfectly executed and preserved than this, with every shingle in place.

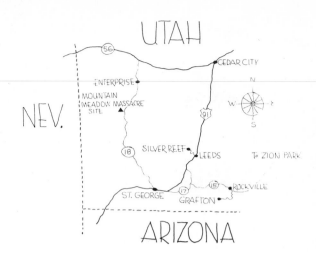

Utah

TROUBLE ON THE MORMON FRONT

Grafton, Utah

Young Mrs. Tenny was in labor. Another Mormon was about to appear to draw life-giving air into its infant lungs and add itself to the flock of Brigham Young's helpers. But why in the name of Moroni, asked the men of Zion in the farming community of Grafton, did this contrary female pick this particular time to have a baby?

The Virgin River was carrying with it all the drainage from torrents of rain washing down the red rock walls and the muddy currents were swirling around and into the Tenny cabin. What to do about this woman in pain? There was no choice.

So the men waded into the knee-deep flood, lifted the bed as the baby was born. The boy henceforth carried the name Marvelous Flood Tenny.

At the general conference of the church in Salt Lake City October, 1861, Brigham Young made a pronouncement to 309 "units," northern colonists going out to settle in the south of Utah. They were to raise cotton as a main crop and families as a second. Most of the units consisted of families but all single men were advised to marry—and at once. When they reached Dixie, as the southern area was called, there would be no women available, and even if there were, even if their sweethearts fol-

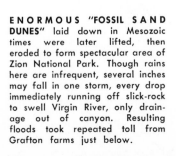

ENORMOUS "FOSSIL SAND DUNES" laid down in Mesozoic times were later lifted, then eroded to form spectacular area of Zion National Park. Though rains here are infrequent, several inches may fall in one storm, every drop immediately running off slick-rock to swell Virgin River, only drainage out of canyon. Resulting floods took repeated toll from Grafton farms just below.

TELEPHOTO LENS dramatizes bold vertical lines of mountain and gaunt adobe structure. Mormon authorities say it served as school, meeting house for prayers, church affairs, social gatherings, was never consecrated temple or church. Unique, historic structure is domed to collapse in few years, shingles on roof decaying, blowing off. Rains, though infrequent here, are heavy and destructive to soft, unfired adobe. Interior is already gutted and cattle roam in and out at will.

lowed them, no marriage would be performed. They must take place in Salt Lake City.

Following the leader's edict emigrants began leaving homes so recently established, some couples almost strangers, others knowing each other only on the trek from Nauvoo, Illinois. One hastily married pair was Nathan C. Tenny and his bride.

The Tennys and several other settlers eventually found themselves established on land close to the Virgin, about six miles above the town of the same name. One account says the new settlement was called Grafton after the Massachusetts town while an old timer in the area told the author a Mr. Grafton was among the settlers and several of his descendants still live around Escalante, Utah.

To the north across the Virgin towered one of Zion's most splendid peaks, Kinesava, an area which would one day become a national park. Young had informed all settlers this would be their "Zion," a statement taken to refer literally to the surrounding mountains. When he visited the colonies along the canyon later he told them the peaks and walls were "not Zion." For years afterward the farmers called the area Not Zion.

When garments brought from Salt Lake City began to fall in shreds replacements were made from wagon covers and tent cloth. These protected modesty and gave some warmth but were harsh to the skin, rough seams rubbing against flesh unprotected by underwear. In a few years small foundation flocks of sheep were producing large amounts of wool, the spinning wheels and carding combs brought in the wagons being put to use. Fleeces were sheared, washed, picked and carded, the wool made into rolls, spun into yarn and woven into cloth, all by slow hand labor.

By 1862 cotton had become a staple crop, the larger towns in the new Dixie surrounded by yellow-bloomed fields. Washington, for example, was planting 140 acres annually, the much smaller Grafton with 28 families growing about an acre each. The home spun clothing was a far greater comfort but there was luxury to come.

Brigham Young encouraged any planting which

SPECTACULAR SCENE once utilized by motion picture company as background for current epic. Mock store, saloon were erected between existing buildings, later removed. Virgin River flows immediately behind them. In background is Mount Kinesava, outer rampart of present Zion National Park. Overhanging trees are old Mulberries, planted by early Mormons in effort to produce silk, leaves being natural food of silkworm.

might produce a food product and one "exotic" plant cultured for utility purposes was the mulberry tree, very likely the so-called Russian variety which is more hardy than some. The blackberry-like fruit, while edible, has the disadvantage of dropping when ripe. One Dixie colonist, a Mrs. Jackson, botanist and plantswoman at heart, carried cuttings and seeds of the mulberry to her new home and soon had a small grove of trees.

The settled part of the country was being swept by a "silkworm craze," speculation sending silkworm eggs to unheard of prices. Rumors of easy success and fantastic profits seeped even into remote southern Utah and Dixie settlers wrote to Brigham Young for permission to produce silk. He not only approved of the venture but in 1874 saw

to it eggs were imported from the Orient and sent to St. George, center of the colonies, for wide distribution.

Pinhead-sized eggs arrived in flats of newspapers and were sprinkled on shredded mulberry leaves from Mrs. Jackson's trees. When 1/4" hatchlings grew to 3" they spun around themselves the essential product, cocoons of silk. Scanty instructions sent with egg shipments led to the eventual production of cloth and finally a silk dress. In later years silk production became an essential industry in Washington County but Grafton shared little in wool, cotton or silk success being too busy trying to fight off the ravages of floods and Indians.

The original settlement was washed away the first year, the colonists moving about a mile up-

RESIDENCE dating from 1870s, well built by Mormons. Thought was given to appearance, situated as it was on corner, far side and front faced with plaster, rear and right squared log walls less eloquent, less conspicuous. Tree at left is one of numerous Mulberries remaining from days of silkworm culture.

stream. At first they called the location New Grafton, later dropping the adjective. Here there was a wider shelf of arable ground, the elevation somewhat higher, but bitter experience had taught them to build ditches, levees and canals. Nevertheless the first spring rains and suddenly melting snows on the heights washed away the hand-built levees and filled ditches with mud and sand.

Even when hungry waters were not carrying away crops and homes Grafton settlers could not afford to relax. Indian attacks were so frequent constant guard was required and the rocky cemetery was filled almost entirely with arrow victims (see *Tales the Western Tombstones Tell*). The steady attrition of fields and men so reduced the once independent Grafton that the remains became a part of Rockville Ward two miles upstream. During the worst of the Indian trouble Grafton was entirely abandoned.

In 1868, with an uneasy peace established, the former Grafton settlers returned to plant grain and cotton once more, the sheep and cattle saved starting new herds. By 1877 there were enough Saints to again organize an independent ward with Alonzo H. Russell as bishop. He acted for ten years when he was succeeded by James Munroe Ballard. In 1900 William Isom took over until 1903 when Ballard was returned as bishop.

Although Indian raids ceased to be a problem the Virgin rose each year with increasing destructiveness and in 1907 so many families moved away the ward was again disorganized, only enough people remaining to justify the residence of Philetus Jones acting as presiding elder. When he went to Rockville as bishop in 1921 Grafton ceased to be a unit of the church.

In succeeding years the town retained two or three families attempting to eke out an existence for a year or two, then abandoning the struggle as hopeless. In 1950 the site was used by a motion picture firm to make a film using the ready-made "set" and picturesque background. When actors and crew left Grafton became a true ghost.

LITTLE PRIDE of construction shown in this building used for sheltering stock.

SILVER IN SANDSTONE

Silver Reef, Utah

The lone prospector was wandering over the bleak ridges searching for metallic color. He was sure the sandstone reefs which stretched everywhere were hopeless but he had to keep moving because it was intensely cold and night was coming on. He reached the Mormon settlement of Leeds after dark but a cheerfully glowing lamp in a window led him to a hospitable family who made him welcome and threw more fuel on the fireplace blaze. The wanderer gratefully warmed his chilled body and as he watched the fire closely he was astonished to see a tiny shining stream ooze from an overheated rock. He caught the drops and later confirmed his belief they were silver.

The extraordinary fact that a tremendous wealth of silver was extracted from sandstone ore at the mining camp of Silver Reef has spawned a dozen different stories to explain the original discovery. The above tale is one of the most frequently repeated but early settler Mark Pendleton gives a different version as being more authentic. In 1878 when he was 14 his family moved from the old home at Parowan to the clamoring town of Silver Reef. He lived there thirteen impressionable years, absorbing everything he saw and heard, and in his reminiscences preserved in Utah's history archives is the following version.

Not far across the Utah-Nevada state line was the notorious mining town of Pioche (see *Tales the Western Tombstones Tell*). Among its several assayers was one called "Metalliferous" Murphy for his congenial optimism about values he saw in ore samples, not always proven accurate Pioche prospectors maintained. Over drinks in a bistro one night miners were discussing Murphy and his "exaggerated" assays and one man exclaimed. "I'll bet Murphy would report silver in a grindstone!" Alcohol promoted this idea into action. A broken grindstone was salvaged and smashed into bits which were duly submitted to Murphy for assay.

True to prediction, Murphy reported the fragments contained silver to the value of 200 ounces per ton and the miners exploded. They gave Murphy a choice between leaving town or being strung up to Pioche's hanging tree. Considering the situation untenable, the assayer chose to leave but braved danger by staying long enough to find out where the samples of stone came from. It seemed the grinding wheel was one of those produced by Isaac Duffing Jr. of Toquerville, Utah, and further tracking put the original chunk of sandstone at the spot where the camp of Silver Reef sprang up. If Murphy made a claim the fact is not recorded but he must have drawn attention to the area. The district was "located" in October of 1876 and by February had over 1000 inhabitants. Although miners, geologists and metallurgists confirmed what the Pioche miners stated, "You can't get silver out of sandstone," the camp produced $9 million in silver between 1877 and 1903, this with the price averaging $1.19 per ounce.

It is generally believed that prospector John Kemple was the first man to actually break off and assay a sample of the reef. His little portable furnace showed a tiny button of silver, not a showing to cause him to throw his hat in the air. He continued on to Nevada but could not forget the strange occurrence of even a little silver in this kind of rock. Kemple later returned with friends, filed a claim and started the Harrisburg Mining District.

A few years later, in 1874, Elijah Thomas and John S. Ferris staked a claim near Leeds on the same formation as Kemple's, of red and white sandstone. Their samples sent to Salt Lake City so

REMAINS of old Spanish arrastra are quite well preserved considering antiquity. When in operation rock-paved disc was centered by post holding up one end of bar or pipe. Over this was slipped stone grinding wheel to about midway point, burro-hitched to outer end. Animal plodded in circle, pulled bar, rolling stone over selected silver ore shoveled in path. Though process was crude, this and countless other similar arrastras served to crush ore until advent of stamp mills.

WELLS FARGO & CO. building is best preserved of structures remaining in Silver Reef, partly because of sturdy construction of dressed sandstone, partly because it has been occupied for years. Town has no inhabitant now except horned toads and rattlesnakes. Iron door shutters are reminiscent of those in California's Mother Lode except for rounded instead of square tops.

excited bankers that they staked William Tecumseh Barbee to head a small group including an assayer to investigate the area. Barbee and his men went to work on the reef but back in Salt Lake all experts advised bank officials they were wasting their money in backing the project, that they considered finding silver in sandstone fantastic, impossible. Barbee was told he was on his own but he decided to stick it out for a while.

He hired a man to haul wood, the heavy iron-rimmed wheels of a loaded wagon skidding and scraping off a long layer of the sandstone surface of what was now called Barbee Reef. Plainly visible was a deposit of hornsilver. The teamster rushed to his boss with the story which Barbee soon confirmed. He set up a camp on the flat nearby, calling it Bonanza City, and wrote to the Salt Like *Tribune*, Feb. 7, 1876, "This sandstone country beats all the boys, and it is amusing to see how excited they all get when they go round to see the sheets of silver which are exposed all over the different reefs. . . . This is the most unfavorable looking country for mines that I have ever seen . . . but as the mines are here, what are the rock sharps going to do about it?"

Barbee made another camp on flats near his Tecumseh mine but a merchant, Hyrum Jacobs, who came from Pioche to set up a store, chose a site where roads from Buckeye, White, Middle and East Reefs came together. Other businesses followed and the new center was named Silver Reef.

Mark Pendleton recalled the day he rode with his parents into the town. As the wagon entered the area he was awed. "To a boy from the tiny village of Parowan, Silver Reef was a big city," he wrote. "The brightly lighted stores and saloons, streets filled with peddlers, freighters' wagons loaded with ore or cordwood on their way to the stamp mills, all were exciting. Miners with dinner pails, Americans, Cornishmen, Irishmen, were walking to the mines where they would spend their ten hours a day."

Silver Reef was essentially a "gentile" town though located almost in the center of the large Mormon settlements in southern Utah, collectively called Dixie. Possibly the most remarkable feature in the history of the mining camp is the equanimity displayed in relations between miners and Mormons. An incident in Rockville, as related in the Mormon-controlled *Under Dixie Sun*, indicated the usual attitude in other nearby areas. "Of course in Rockville as in other communities there were men who obeyed the counsel of church leaders and had taken more than one wife. During the 1870s and '80s the United States Government was trying to punish those who were practicing the law of their religion. The Saints felt that they were . . . entitled to live their religion as they pleased. When the Marshal came to Rockville or Grafton a messenger was sent up the river to warn the people so they would have a chance to hide all those who where in danger as second or third wives. . . . On April 21 they came and took Fanny Slaughter. . . . They tried her in court before a jury but could not get a conviction on the charge of polygamy.

"Their hatred of the Saints was so vehement that they were determined to convict her on some

BUSINESS BUILDINGS north of Wells Fargo offices were constructed with less care, are now largely falling into complete ruin. This impressive relic facing setting sun is reputed to have been Chinese Drug Store. Sandstone blocks, erected before days of efficient silver extraction, contain large percentage of precious metal. Such buildings in other mining camps were demolished and run through mills. With present increasing values in white metal these evidences of glory days in Silver Reef could suffer same fate.

charge or other. She was postmistress in Rockville at the time, and when her accounts were gone over it was found they were short three cents. As Sister Slaughter started to walk from the courtroom she was stopped by an officer and again arrested, this time for 'defrauding the United States Mail.'"

In contrast to this bitterness a brief Mormon history told of differences between Silver Reef miners and the people of Leeds just below. When water was suddenly released at Silver Reef, inundating farms at Leeds and washing out ditches, "miners gladly came to assist Leeds people in repairing their ditches, and in turn elders of Leeds would often be called to Silver Reef to preach at funerals."

Indefatigable writer Barbee included an item in the *Tribune*. "They (the Mormons) have a very hard time serving the Lord in this desert, a god-forsaken looking country. It is about time something turned up to take the place of sorghum wine as a circulating medium." He was of course referring to the stream of silver his mine was then pouring forth. The *Tribune's* circulation must have extended to St. George, Mormon center of Dixie. Shortly after Barbee's self-congratulatory letter ap-

peared in print Apostle Erastus Snow observed at Sunday services, "Now that Brother Barbee has turned up something to bring prosperity to Dixie let us pray for God's blessing on him for opening up the mines."

Carrying brotherly love even further, Father Scanlon, priest of the large Catholic Church at Silver Reef, was invited to serve Mass in the Mormon Tabernacle at St. George on a certain Sunday. In unprecedented fashion the congregation learned the Latin ritual chants beforehand so as to assist in the services. And when Federal officers on their way to St. George to arrest polygamists stopped at Silver Reef overnight, the Mormon telegraph operator would order "two chairs" from the furniture store in the county seat, thus alerting the Saints there.

The silver camp's several saloons were noted for fine quality liquor . . . all but one, that is. That was a bargain shop attracting cheap buyers. After complaints about the whiskey it was discovered the proprietor "stretched" the contents of the barrels with a witches' brew of tobacco, strychnine and water.

For a change from whiskey, good and bad,

miners would go down to Leeds to have Sunday dinner at the hospitable boarding house where the famous and potent red Mormon wine was generously served. Regular imbibers took it in stride but incautious miners were often hauled away in what Pendleton describes as "an unconscious condition and waking up to wonder what had happened."

As in most mining camps frequent fires raged uncontrolled and took a big toll. One of the worst razed most of the town in 1879. In double file citizens passed powder kegs from buildings to creeks and back again. The Chinese cook in Kate Duggery's restaurant was credited with saving that building by snatching up an open can of milk and dousing out the sparks.

The town maintained a race track during its prosperous years where visitors from St. George gathered with their blooded horses raised in the Kanab region. Segregated from the elite were Indians in paint and feathers, prospectors in working garb, tinhorn and professional gamblers in ruffled silk shirts. And farthest from the track were the dance hall girls and other mining camp flotsam.

Inevitably the days of big time money drew to an end, the process so gradual few people recognized it. As silver production and values "temporarily" eased off, miners' wages were dropped from a daily $4 to $3. Resentful men organized and retaliated with strikes and sabotage. In 1881 the situation was so out of hand authorities called for help in controlling violence. Sheriff A. P. Hardy rounded up 25 men, assembling them at Leeds. Since most of them were members of the Mormon Church, St. George Stake President John D. McAllister sent a written message of instructions to Hardy:

"We view with alarm the assembly of 25 Saints for this purpose and extend you these cautions. Have total abstinence from anything intoxicating. Studiously observe your posse, should the brethren seem fatigued, a cup of coffee is recommended. Do not stray away from each other, nor visit saloons or gambling halls. Keep together and be on the watch. All attend to prayers in the morning and at night before retiring."

An unusually heavy snowstorm covered readying operations at Leeds allowing Hardy and his men to surprise the insurrectionists at camp and arrest 36 of them. The town's tiny jail being inadequate for the prisoners they were confined in the solid stone dance hall. The next day they were taken to Beaver for trial, the sheriff reporting the trip a "miserable affair," with passengers in open wagons soaked in a cold rain mixed with snow.

Silver Reef experienced the usual murders expected in an unrestricted mining camp (some described in *Boot Hill*). One is commemorated by a beautifully carved tombstone in the camp's cemetery, placed on the grave of Michael Garbis by his son, Michael Jr. The father was slain by a discharged employee who was tried in St. George and found guilty, the execution thwarted by a mob that snatched him from the jail and hanged him at the edge of town. The hanging rope was tied to a bush so that the body was left swinging on the tree. Passing the spot the next morning, the town wag was reported to have said, "I have observed that tree growing there for the last 25 years. This is the first time I have ever seen it bearing fruit."

SILVER REEF is located in area of spectacular desert scenery. Plants here must be of type capable of storing water supplied only in short rainy season. Most conspicuous around old silver camp are cacti of **Opuntia** tribe, this species flaunting satiny blossoms of brilliant chartreuse hue. At right of Wells Fargo & Co. is seen typical plant group, detail of flowers shown here.

JOHNNIE TOWN is at bottom of grade below mine, conveniently located beside Nevada State 16. Stone building shown and several frame buildings still stand. Some years ago, Charles Labbe, owner of Labbe mine, also located above town, described Johnnie Town as having "several good houses and one fine tree."

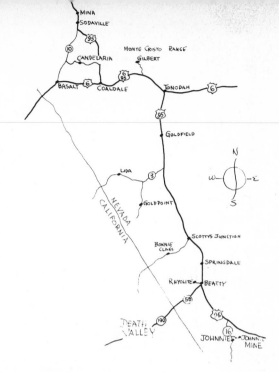

Nevada

SAGA OF THE "LOST BREYFOGLE"

Johnnie, Nevada

Prospector Breyfogle lost a mine he never had. More accurately he could not find the place where he picked up the rich chunk of gold. He made many searches, all to no avail, and broken in health and spirit, he died in the desert. But at least ten rich mines east and north of Death Valley have been identified as the "Lost Breyfogle." Was the real one the Johnnie?

The road up to the large Labbe mine is rough but passable and old time Nevada miner Charles Labbe has been studying the Breyfogle story for many years. He believes he knows about what happened to Jacob (or Louis Jacob or C. C. Jacob or Byron W.) Breyfogle, the events before and after his death.

He says that around 1861 Breyfogle brought a fantastically rich chunk of ore into the thriving mining center of Austin, Nevada. He was barely alive, desiccated and near starvation but was able to say he found the sample somewhere in or near the eastern edge of Death Valley. As soon as he was able to eat and walk he started the first of many searches.

In 1865 a party was following the old Spanish Trail from California to Salt Lake. At a camping ground called Stump Springs, not far from where Johnnie would later be established, they came upon Breyfogle who had barely survived an attack by Indians. He was taken on to Salt Lake where he was nursed by one "Pony" Duncan. He regained a

measure of health and took Duncan as partner on another hunt for gold. They had hardly made a good beginning when Breyfogle died, first confiding all he knew of his lost "mine" to Duncan. Later Duncan met the Montgomery brothers who were also looking for it and they pooled information.

In 1890 George and Robert Montgomery were camped at Indian Spring Ranch when they hired Indian Johnnie as guide. The Paiute took them almost directly to some veins with exposed gleams of gold. Excited at first, the Montgomerys cooled down when they found the gold in view was all of it, not enough to warrant the hauling of supplies and equipment to the remote spot. Then Indian Johnnie said something like, "Well all right then, I'll take you about four miles south of here where there is a quartz ledge really loaded with gold." About an hour later the party stood before what Charles Labbe says, "was either the Breyfogle or at least what was the nearest among many versions of the lost mine."

Robert Montgomery later reported the gold in the decomposed surface of quartz was like "plums in a pudding." It was this display of nuggets that gave the location the name "Chispas," literally Spanish for "sparks" or "diamonds," but locally meaning gold nuggets. The mine was rich enough, producing some $250,000 by 1899 when the ledge pinched out. In the meantime another, richer and longer lasting, find was made on the steep hill to

FAMOUS OLD JOHNNIE MINE, for many years beset by turbulence, bloodshed, killings. Ore was dumped directly into mill at left, tailings seen in left middle distance. View looks north toward Mt. Sterling, other peaks. Area is entirely unforested but has scanty covering of desert vegetation.

126

DECAYING HOUSES in Johnnie. Photo made from porch of one directly below, for a few months occupied by Kathryn and Bob West. Tangled remains of chicken wire was once neatly stretched, bore blooming annual vines that gave shade, color to bleak cabins.

the east. The town growing up near the Chispas and the new mine as well were named for the Indian guide. To avoid confusion the village became Johnnie Town, active workings above Johnnie mine.

After treating a hundred tons of ore at the new mine it was evident more equipment would be justified, so a 10-stamp mill was erected, its boilers at first fired by yucca stems. During those first months all machinery and supplies had to be hauled over desert roads 140 miles from Daggett. Later a railroad came to Barnwell, 100 miles to the southeast, a stage line starting from there.

Historian Harvey Hardy writes that sometime around 1900 the Johnnie mining claim was leased by a company with headquarters in Salt Lake City,

the officials mostly Mormons. When their lease ran out, the Montgomery manager whose name Hardy remembers as McArthur, refused an extension. Jerry Langford, manager for the Salt Lake concern, was determined to retain the mine against all comers, including the legal owners.

While armed guards protected them, Langford's miners continued to take out rich ore. One night a force was assembled by McArthur on the hill directly above the mine, among it such gunfighters as Phil Foote and Jack Longstreet. In the early morning light, before guards were stationed, McArthur's men opened fire on the miners going to work, routing and scattering them in every direction as long as it was downhill.

The legal owners then moved in and immediately

MAIN STREET of Johnnie mine looking up slope in approximately southerly direction.

began mining operations. When several days passed without incident, the gunmen relaxed vigilance and all guards were taken off. This was the signal for the enemy to take over the same hill from which they had been evicted and start shooting. In the reversed situation McArthur's men ran to the hoist house for cover. After suffering several casualties they were ready to give up but for a time were unable to find something to serve as a flag of surrender. Then the squaw of Jack Longstreet was found among the beleaguered and her white petticoat was tied to a rifle and effective in putting an end to hostilities.

Most seriously wounded among McArthur's men was Phil Foote who was suffering much pain. A man was sent to Johnnie Town to get morphine and after a record trip returned with storekeeper Sam Yount who administered the drug. The suffering man went to sleep, "permanently," as Hardy recalls.

According to this account, the Mormons continued to operate the Johnnie mine for some years, then ran into financial difficulties. Miners were not paid regularly and threatened to quit. With bills for services and supplies mounting the officials sent to headquarters for help.

From Salt Lake City came a man named Gillespie with money to settle outstanding debts which was totally inadequate and in the hassle as to who would get what money there was, Gillespie was killed by a shotgun blast. The town blacksmith was accused and taken to Belmont, Nye County seat, for trial but released for lack of evidence.

Charles Labbe's account of the trouble is terse. "The leasers wanted to jump the claim for themselves and all hell broke loose. Two men, Phil Foote and a man named Gillespie were killed, the mill burned down and office blown up. I picked up the safe, minus the door, 200 feet away." He recalls the dead were buried at Pahrump, not far away and that no trial was ever held.

In 1905 a Los Angeles concern took over the

Johnnie mine and production continued moderately until 1908. The "Happy Hunch" whose real name was Ed Overfield, hailing from Goldfield, led an exploratory drilling operation nearby that uncovered a vein three feet wide and assaying $30,000 in gold to the ton. Reporters from Salt Lake's *Mining Review* looked and hurried back to spread the sensational news. Labbe says he saw one chunk from the vein from which $20 gold pieces could be cut. Unfortunately the lead soon ran into Johnnie mine ground and operations ceased.

The Johnnie ran along on an extension of a "pocket zone" until 1940 when the owner died. In a year or so there was further activity by another Los Angeles promoter but when drilling produced no substantial leads, quiet again settled down on the old camp (see *Tales the Western Tombstones Tell*).

JOHNNIE MINE saw several alternating periods of desertion, activity. In 1941 two Hollywood, Calif. men, Joe De Grazier and Walter Knott, promoted reopening of mine with money "invested" for wealthy widow of movie capital. They hired mining expert Robert West, several other knowledgeable men to clean out shaft. "Bob" West and wife Kathryn set up housekeeping in old building still in fair condition. Activity was feverish for 3 months until authorities discovered De Grazier, Knott had mismanaged funds, depleted almost all before actual mining could start. Without waiting for outcome of shady affair, West quit, left for home. Promoters later received jail sentences. Photo of then active post office was made with old Eastman folding Kodak by Kathryn West. After closure office was moved to Pahrump in valley.

ENDS OF BOARDS in porch of old Columbus Hotel show extreme weathering.

GOLCONDA, 15 miles east of Winnemucca, is very ghostly now, but when Midas gold mines were operating it was busy as a supply center for miners there. Altho the center of Golconda Mining District, surrounding mines were never spectacular, biggest strike coming in 1930s with development of multiple-metal Getchell mine after Golconda had become near ghost. 26-mile distant Getchell produced tungsten, gold, molybdenum. Photo shows rooming-boarding house at Golconda. Old cemetery is nearby, well worth visit. Small grocery store still operates.

SUPPLY CENTER ON THE TRUCKEE

Wadsworth, Nevada

To those weary travelers plodding toward California's golden El Dorado, the stopping place on the green banks of a river called Truckee was heaven on earth. Many of those who spent searing weeks in crossing the sands of the Great Basin plunged their dehydrated bodies into the river's clear waters. Twenty years later this welcome oasis was the site of a settlement, Wadsworth.

The Truckee is only 105 miles long. Beginning as a clear mountain stream in the High Sierra, over 6,000 feet above sea level, fed by waters overflowing from Lake Tahoe, it ends decimated by irrigation usage as a thick, silt-laden dribble in brackish Pyramid Lake. Famed Chief Winnemucca was said to have a son named Truckee and called the river that in his honor. However the Spanish name for trout is *trucha*, and as the river was called the Salmon Trout by Capt. John Fremont, that may be the true derivation of the name.

The Truckee makes its last sharp turn a few miles south of its end. Just north of Wadsworth it enters Pyramid Lake Reservation, established by President Grant March 23, 1874, for benefit of the Paiute inhabitants of the region. They lived largely on fish, especially the enormous cutthroat trout teeming in the river and Pyramid Lake. What they could not eat they sold to immigrants and later settlers.

The place once called the "Big Bend" is about 2,000 feet below the point where the Truckee emerges from Lake Tahoe. It was here Fremont left the stream he paralleled while descending the steep slopes of the Sierra in January, 1844, and where the pioneers taking this route west stopped, rested and then forded at a point just below the bend, a shallow place they termed "Lower Crossing." Some without the courage to climb over the mountain barricade called High Sierra, stayed and built shanties, living on fish and game while their stock grew fat on luxuriously growing grass. No town or settlement of any size resulted however until the advent of the Central Pacific Railroad.

The spot was a strategic one for the railroad. For the push east across a vast expanse of desert there would be no more wood or water for the engines. So at first Wadsworth served as a supply depot in the building of the line, then in 1868 became a permanent and important station. Settlers there now made a comfortable living cutting and hauling wood from fringes of the timbered mountains and the tenuous town became solid. Stores were established, hotels, saloons and gambling places sprouted like mushrooms as railroad building and maintenance crews roistered. Car shops for the Truckee division, extending from Truckee to Winnemucca, were located at the river's bend. These with work shops steadily employed a large number of men, roundhouse containing twenty stalls.

As soon as the railroad was completed to this point it became the base for supplies to mines then active to the south in Churchill, Nye and Esmeralda Counties. An old *History of Nevada* reads, "The excellent roads leading to Ellsworth, Columbus, Belmont and other towns are lined with long freight teams conveying goods and supplies from Wadsworth. As long as those points are supplied by freight wagons, Wadsworth will get the bulk of the traffic, but as soon as one of the proposed railroads invades that region the freighting business will materially decline. At the present time the population of about 500 are busy and prosperous."

For two years Wadsworth was a bone of contention between Washoe and Lyon Counties because of boundary uncertainties. It had been assumed the line followed the "old emigrant road" but the people of Lyon County discovered traces of a "cut off" which they insisted was the main route. If conceded this would leave Wadsworth in Lyon County which they wanted. Jurisdiction over Wadsworth had always been exercised by Washoe authorities and with Lyon's brazen attempt to take over a rich source of tax money, they took the matter to court. The case was tried twice in Ormsby County without arriving at a solid decision. A third attempt in Humboldt County cleared the matter for Washoe in 1871.

For some reason the section of railroad in the vicinity of Wadsworth was accident prone. The most spectacular near-disaster from the point of casualties was on June 13, 1872. Passenger car No. 1 passed over a broken rail six miles west of town. The two rear coaches jumped the track but plunged on, held upright by the rocky walls of the cut, dragged along to the end of it where they leaped down and were demolished. Had they tipped the other way they would have rolled into the canyon of the Truckee with great loss of life. As it was no one was killed although many were seriously injured.

COLUMBUS HOTEL, long abandoned, and little church with tottering weather vane stand alone in what was busy part of town. It was founded by overland emigrants on their way to California gold fields, stimulated by coming of railroad, nurtured as supply center for booming camps just south of Wadsworth. Collapse came with inevitable failure of mining camps to survive.

"HANG ON TO IT, SANDY"

Gold Hill, Nevada

You could say "Old Virginia" Finney had two loves—his home state of Virginia and Forty-rod whiskey. He deserted the first but fell hard for the amber lightning. Once he stumbled at his desert camp, breaking the flask of whiskey in his hip pocket. He gazed ruefully at the dark spot on the ground and decided some use should be made of it. Scattering broken glass over the stain he intoned, "I christen this spot Virginia."

John Bishop's modest discovery of gold up the canyon from Johntown sparked the larger exploration of Nevada which was to some extent still unknown to man. Without Gold Canyon, Nevada's vast stores of mineral wealth might have remained under the ground for many years. Certainly the "fine dust" Bishop saw in the bottom of his pan eventually led to the later discoveries farther up the hill and the founding of Virginia City, most fabulous mining camp of all time, largely instrumental in saving the Civil War for the Union.

Old Johntown, long since utterly vanished, was a cluster of saloons, honky-tonks and shacks near the mouth of Gold Canyon and not far from where Dayton was later established. It was a hangout for prospectors and drifters of all kinds. In the summer of 1859 men were swarming all over the surrounding hills, including Sun Peak (later Mt. Davidson). No spectacular discoveries were made but enough to warrant further search. Autumn brought a heavy freeze followed by continuous cold, all streams freezing solid, stopping all pan-

GOLD HILL BAR AND HOTEL flourished with mine production, ups and downs reflected in patronage, gambling tables. Sustained prosperity was maintained for 20 years, 1868-88. Records show Yellow Jacket mine poured forth $14 million, Crown King $11, adjoining Belcher $15,397,200 in dividends. Old stone and brick structure is still solid. Turned balusters on balcony are originals. Much plaster has fallen from walls, exposing field stone.

ning and sluicing attempts. Everybody retired to Johntown to spend the winter.

Toward the end of January there was a general thaw that sent water running in all the gulches. Men suffering from cabin fever and satiated with the pleasures of the flesh headed up Gold Canyon, the party that included John Bishop having a certain place in mind, a rocky knoll on the west side just north of where Gold Hill would be established.

Bishop later wrote, "Where Gold Hill now stands I had noticed indications of a ledge and had got a little color. I spoke to 'Old Virginia' about it and he said he remembered the locality, that he had often noticed it when out hunting for deer and antelope. He also said he had seen any quantity of quartz, so he joined our party and Comstock also followed along. When we got to the ground I took a pan and filled it with dirt with my foot as I had no shovel or spade." Bishop took the pan to a cluster of willows on the creek. "There was considerable gold left in the bottom, very fine, like flour," he said. "Old Virginia decided that it was a good place to begin work."

The immediate problem was water enough to wash the gold dust and Old Virginia Finney appointed himself the one to go look. He set off up the canyon while, as Bishop told it, "I and my partner meantime had a talk together, and decided to put the others of our party in the middle of the good ground." When Finney returned with the news he had located ample water and learned he had been omitted from these plans he was under-standably irked. He made some bitter remarks and added, "Well, if you boys are going to hog it all go ahead. I'm going to make my own strike." However he must have changed his mind for when the claims were laid out to be staked, he took his along with the rest. When the men conferred on a name all at first favored Gold Canyon but since the strike was on a hill, the name would be Gold Hill.

Other prospectors sniffed at Bishop's find. The dust was so fine it was hardly worth bothering with, they said. But when the dirt was worked up to a point where a rotted ledge of quartz was uncovered it became evident the boys had a bonanza, foreseen by the astute Bishop. Johntown unbelievers widened their eyes when Gold Hill takes grew from $5 a day per man to $15, then $25. Then came the rush with the men camping under small trees all along the canyon, then in shanties and then log houses. Gold Hill could now be called a reality.

Another celebrated personality of Gold Hill was Allison "Eilley" Orrum Hunter Cowan Bowers who had progressed from her native Scotland to the camp by a devious route. When Eilley reached her fifteenth birthday she became a Mormon convert at the urging of Stephen Hunter who was proselyting in the old country. It turned out Hunter had more in mind than converting the attractive lassie. He ran off with her to Nauvoo, Illinois, the Mormon stronghold in America, and married her in the church.

GOLD HILL city fathers were once so optimistic as to introduce act in Territorial Legislature to put up state capital building on level spot near town. Prosperity in mining camps was largely gauged by price of drinks in saloons. 10-cent shot indicated camp of small respect and when bars in Gold Hill began charging "two bits" for slug of redeye, high rating of town was acknowledged.

Fires periodically ravaged thriving camp, one in Yellow Jacket mine erupting April 7, 1869, most sombre day in town's history. Combined fire fighting forces of communities failed over flames roaring thru underground tunnels. 33 men died, only 27 bodies recovered. Some fires smoldered 3 years.

Another fire in 1873 killed 4, injured 11. These ruins were left when ground level flames gutted interior. Though then doing little business post office managed to operate until Feb. 27, 1943. Years before that drinks in saloons were reduced to 10 cents, Gold Hill News editor remarking, "With nothing but ten cent saloons in town we might as well suspend," and did just that.

All went well with the romance until Hunter took a second wife under the policy of bigamy. Eilley's was an independent spirit not tolerating a second woman in her husband's bed and during preparations for the epic Mormon migration to Utah, the ex-Mrs. Hunter met and married young Alexander Cowan.

The Cowans had barely settled themselves in Salt Lake when they were sent still farther west to help colonize the valleys near Mormon Genoa in Nevada. Then once again plans were interrupted. The United States threatened to send troops against the Mormons and Brigham Young called back all scattered settlers in far flung places. Eilley's new husband was eager to respond but not his Scottish spouse. She was sick of repeated expeditions forced by the church and bade her second husband goodbye. She remained in Nevada.

In Johntown Eilley started a boarding house that was successful from the start because of her good Scotch cooking. She followed the mass evacuation to Gold Hill and set up her business there. Among the boarders was young Sandy Bowers who attracted her despite his being fourteen years younger and she began showing him favors of several varieties, eventually marrying him. It was gossiped about by other boarders that Sandy had run up a big board bill and was vulnerable to the lady's proposal. His present to the bride was a strip of "dirt" alongside his own early established claim.

Married life was just under way when the diggings began to fail generally with the result that the more easily discouraged sold out. Mrs. Bowers persuaded Sandy not to capitulate but rather buy some of the now cheap claims. The rest is history. While others lost their holdings the Bowers sud-

BANK OF CALIFORNIA was branch of main office in Virginia City, short distance above on Sun Mountain. Intense rivalry existed between towns. To escape being overwhelmed by larger VC thru greedy operators who wished to grab Gold Hill's support for building sidewalks, gas, sewers, street lights, other improvements in VC without benefit to GH, it incorporated Dec. 17, 1862 gaining victory over faction in legislature featuring its annexation to VC.
Boundaries were described as "on the north by the southern boundary of Virginia City; on the east and south by the boundary line between Storey and Lyon (Counties); on the west by the boundary between Storey and Washoe." Apparently Gold Hill was ever optimistic about wealth underground, permanence of then booming town.

HUGE BOWERS MANSION was built in 1862 at cost of $300,000, largely furnished with expensive appointments bought by the Bowers on triumphal tour of Europe. On return of new-wealthy pair, Sandy Bowers felt uneasy in luxurious aspect, preferred saloons, housekeeping rooms at Gold Hill. When he died there at 35, members of Gold Hill Masonic Lodge conducted his funeral at Fraternal Hall, and in accordance with last wishes to "Follow me as far as you can," population formed procession on horses, in carriages and wagons extending almost solidly down to Bowers' mansion.

Sandy Bowers was laid to rest on hill few yards behind great house he disdained. Later he was joined in death by adopted daughter Persia. Many years later when owner of Bower house heard of Eilley Bowers' death he had her body brought home, placed beside kin. Graves are in brushy area of high fire danger, access denied by authorities.

denly began to take in thousands of dollars a day from their united claims which hit a bonanza. In a few months Eilley and Sandy were millionaires.

With huge wealth now at her disposal Eilley resolved to build a castle that would put to shame anything previously built in Nevada, an easy thing to do since few miners, even fabulously rich ones, wanted permanent homes there. And Eilley dreamed of a grand tour of Europe staging as a finale audience with Queen Victoria.

The great mansion was erected down on the level land near Washoe City (see *Ghost Town*

Album). And off to Europe she and Sandy went, buying splendid furnishings for the great house at every stop, the starry-eyed Mrs. Bowers paying any price asked. She would show those old fogeys in Scotland who had objected to her romance with Hunter what was what, even though Hunter had little to do with her present affluence. The tour was a shining success until she came up against British protocol. Queen Victoria refused to see Eilley, a divorcee.

After two years the Bowers returned home, following a steady stream of marble mantles, gilded French furniture and plush fixtures that had to be shipped around the Horn, then freighted over the High Sierra.

But all this was Eilley's dream come true, not Sandy's. He refused to live permanently in the mansion so lavishly appointed, caring nothing for the glossy society Eilley hoped to gather around her, and rejoined his old cronies in the Gold Hill saloons. Being nothing like astute he allowed his business affairs to become hopelessly muddled and suddenly died in 1868. He was thirty-five years old.

Sadly enough Eilley realized little from the claims when sold due to litigation and accumulated debts, although the properties were potentially very valuable. The widow, once so natively canny, became strangely trustful and careless. Before long it was necessary to mortgage the immense house and retire from public entertaining and ostentatious display. Too late she reversed her spending, making one last extravagant gesture—the purchase of a large crystal ball.

Acting on advice from the sphere she attempted to run the mansion as an elegant resort which involved cook and maid services for the paying guests. When there was no money left to pay them, they left and Eilley reverted to her former status as cook, maid and laundress. When she could talk her guests into it she told their fortunes with the aid of her crystal ball.

Apparently by not interpreting her advice correctly, one man lost a fortune in selling a claim that soon proved an El Dorado. The incident did much to undermine any reputation Mrs. Bowers retained. The activity of seeress and other sources of income fell off to nothing, the one-time millionairess was left broke and starving. She sold the house to a wealthy man who pitied her enough to allow her to stay as scullery maid and janitress, but Eilley was unable to scrub floors any more. She was discharged and drifted away to die in 1903, a ragged, lonely old woman.

BOWERS MANSION had advantage of high-priced architects, builders. Stone cutters were likely Cornish "Cousin Jacks" rightly reputed to be best in world. Stone blocks were so well trimmed little or no mortar was necessary. Cracks shown here were caused by severe earthquake that shook down magnificent ruin of Withington Hotel in ghost town of Hamilton (see **Western Ghost Towns**).

In 1873 State of Nevada had chance to buy Bowers house and surrounding 120 acres for $20,000, contemplating use as insane asylum but deal failed. Much later house and grounds became county park, with picnic area, swimming pool. In 1967 facilities were enlarged. Fortunately mansion itself remains intact, visitors conducted thru faded splendors for small fee.

MONUMENT TO MEMORY of Charles D. Poston, "Father of Arizona," Alcalde of Tubac who died at Phoenix in 1902, was buried there in spite of last request that he rest on summit of Parsee Hill. While on trip to India Poston embraced sun-worshipper faith. Back in Arizona he built expensive road to top of butte near Florence, started "Eternal Fire" on summit. When fire failed after several months residents in area termed peak "Poston's Folly." In 1925 researchers working on Poston history, realizing his importance in early Arizona initiated movement to remove his bones to summit and erect this pyramidal monument. Grave is accessible only on foot over steep trail composed of loose lava clinkers.

Arizona

NO LAW BUT LOVE

Tubac, Arizona

The story of Tubac is interwoven with those of southern Arizona's three most important missions, San Xavier del Bac, Tumacacori and Guevavi (often spelled Guebabi). San Xavier, poetically referred to as the White Dove of the Desert, has been in almost constant use and is possibly the most beautiful and finest example of mission architecture in the United States. Tumacacori, victim of Apaches and vandals, is a pathetic shell, yet retains a certain nobility. Its ruins are arrested from further decay by its present status as a national monument. Guevavi, older and never as large nor as solidly built as the others, has all but disappeared, its adobe walls melted to mere mounds of mud. Of the seven missions established by Father Kino during his service within the present

boundaries of Arizona, only these three were known to have been in operation at the time of his death in 1711.

Missions and ranches of the Tubac area were constantly exposed to murderous Apache raids during their early years and were all but inoperative by 1851. In that year, Pima and Papago tribes joined forces in an earth sweep just north of the Mexican border. Priests who had failed to escape were killed and Spanish silver-mining equipment, in operation since 1736, was destroyed. The next year a presidio, or garrison was established at Tubac, with soldiers offering a measure of protection to what few farmers remained. By 1753, the priests had returned to their devastated churches.

The earliest history of Tubac as a settlement isn't clear, but its name originated from a Pima

SOME GRAVES in old Tubac cemetery are marked but whole sections lack any identification.

word meaning "a burned out place." Located beside the Santa Cruz River, it is bordered on the west by the Diablito Mountains and on the other horizon by the Santa Ritas. The river, now a trickle at best, was a dependable stream in the days of Tubac's prosperity, even justifying the building of grist mills along its banks. By 1776 the town was the center of an extensive farming, cattle raising and mining community. In that year, Anza chose the fertile spot as a gathering place while he planned his push on to San Francisco. Already distinguished as being the oldest town established by white men in Arizona, Tubac became the first Mormon settlement in the state just 100 years later.

Shortly after the arrival of the "Saints," there appeared a man who later would be called the "Father of Arizona." This was Charles D. Poston, who with his friend Herman Ehrenberg prospected the neighboring mountains in 1854. Poston found sufficient indications of mineral wealth to warrant his being chosen to lead an expedition sent out two years later by the Sonora Exploring and Mining Company, which developed into the Heintzelman mine.

During this period, Poston was put in charge of the town's 800 souls, four-fifths of them Mexicans. Invested by his company with the title of Alcalde, the new mayor instigated a unique monetary system in use at Tubac in 1858. Since almost the entire populace was illiterate, paper money called *boletas*, bearing pictures instead of numbered denominations was used. A pig signified 12½ cents, a calf 25c, a rooster 50c, a horse $1.00 and a bull $5.00.

Poston wrote of the community at this time, "We had no law but love and no occupation but labor; no government, no taxes, no public debt, no poli-

RESTORATION at Tubac has been generally well done, building of this wall not finished where lamp post is inserted. Many other adobe buildings need repairing or complete rebuilding. Insertion of wheel in adobe wall is anachronism not appealing to purists.

FRAGMENT of original Mexican Presidio near modern museum. Soldiers stationed here protected residents from vicious Apaches for comparatively short period.

tics. It was a community in a perfect state of nature." So natural were some of the relations between young couples at Tubac—who merely set up housekeeping without benefit of clergy—that Poston inquired the reason. "It's a long journey to the nearest priest," they said, "and the father charges a fee of $25, which we cannot afford."

Poston then took it upon himself to perform marriages, claiming he was legally authorized to do so because of his government position. Instead of charging a stiff fee, Poston performed the rites free, even presenting the happy couples with a gift. In addition to marrying "new" couples, he married many who had already had offspring and wished to make their children legitimate. So popular did this service become that strange faces from surrounding areas began to show up at his office. "I had been marrying people and baptizing children for two years and had a good many god-children named Carlos or Carlotta, according to gender, and had begun to feel quite patriarchal," he commented, when the blow fell.

Bishop Lamy sent down to Tubac a priest named Macbeuf, the Vicar Apostolic of New Mexico. According to the Bishop, Father Macbeuf was to "look after the spiritual condition of the people of Tubac." Extremely conscientious, the priest followed the precepts of church law to the letter. The few sheets in town were commandeered to make walls for a confessional; he made parishioners wait until noon for the breakfast blessing, and he or-

dered that his followers have nothing to do with the Alcalde who had been so grossly encroaching upon the rights of the church. But worse yet, he informed his distraught congregation that marriages and baptisms that had been performed by Poston were illegal, that many were living in adultery. Then, going to Poston, he informed him that he had ordered the sinful cohabitors to suspend connubial relations forthwith.

In his journal, Poston says of the situation: "I knew there would be a riot on the Santa Cruz if this ban could not be lifted. Women sulked; men cursed, maintaining they were entitled to the rights of matrimony. My strong defense was that I had not charged any of them anything and had given them a treat, a marriage certificate with a seal on it made out of a Mexican dollar and had forged on an anvil." Still, though the Pope of Rome was beyond the jurisdiction of even the Alcalde of Tubac, he could not see the way open to a restoration of happiness.

"It would never do to let the population of the Territory be stopped in this way," he continued, "so I arranged with Father Macbeuf to give sanctity of the church to the marriages and legitimatize the little Carlos and Carlottas with holy water at a cost to the company of $700." This rectified the matrimonial situation along the Santa Cruz River and all were again satisfied." (Reprinted by courtesy of *Desert Magazine*.)

DISTILLED FROM BLOOD AND COURAGE

Calabasas, Arizona

Oh yes, the old timer agreed, the Apaches were cruel, ruthless, bold and bloodthirsty. But he knew of one case where 200 of them were bitten by white men's bullets and none ever lived to retaliate. Well, there was proof of that too. Don Frederico Hulseman showed Peter Bady a string of what looked to him like dried apple slices, about three feet long. "Ears, my friend," said Don Frederico, "cut from those dead Apaches. See the gold and beaded earrings?"

In this part of southern Arizona and many areas of the southwest travelers take note of curious, spreading vines, each plant usually covering roughly about ten feet in diameter. Early in the season there will be many blossoms scattered along the vines, replaced in late summer by globular fruits about grapefruit size. When dry they are hollow except for seeds that rattle on shaking, leaves and other succulent parts disappearing to leave the hardshelled globes, now pale straw colored, conspicuous on the vines.

These are the wild form of Cucurbita Pepo, an inedible form of pumpkin. They grow in abundance in southern Arizona. Early Spanish explorers found the vines growing everywhere and in the Indians' field of corn, cultivated pumpkins. They called the village Calabasas, either for the little inedible gourds or table pumpkins. The native vines proved far more enduring and still flourish at the townsite long bare of almost any trace of busy life.

For several years following 1691 Father Kino spent most of his time traveling between his mis-

LONELY REMNANT of adobe building, likely last surviving trace of Calabasas with its dark, bloody history. Searching for old town best directions available led author to spot on banks of dry Santa Cruz River where large field of cotton flourished in full bloom. Spanish speaking Mexican workers disclaimed ever having heard of town but said this patch of cotton was called "Calabasas field." Beating thorny mesquite brush revealed this broken relic.

sion at San Xavier del Bac and the head mission at Dolores, Sonora. As a matter of convenience he later established a second mission at Guevavi (sometimes Guebabi). With a priest station here the Indian village of Calabasas became a more readily accessible *visita*.

In 1767 the Spanish government expelled all Jesuit priests from the new world including the area around Calabasas. By 1827 all Spanish, whether priests or ranch owners were expelled by the now dominant Mexican authorities, leaving missions and *visitas* fully vulnerable to murderous Apaches. Calabasas was reduced to little more than a tiny village, a few Mexicans working a gold mine nearby.

In 1842 the square leagues of land comprising Tumacacori, Calabasas and Guevavi were combined into one huge grant which, two years later, the state of Sonora sold to one Francisco Aguilar for $500. A coincidence that Aguilar was the brother-in-law of Manuel Gandra, Governor of Sonora?

During the next decade Gov. Gandra built and fortified a large hacienda at Calabasas, the most attractive site along the generously flowing Santa Cruz River. He stocked it with huge herds of cattle, horses and sheep, the watching Apaches holding back until the rancho was complete, then moving in for the kill. Driving off all stock for butchering and burning, they slaughtered some Mexicans and put the rest to flight. An American dragoon passing by in 1854 stopped there and later wrote, "... at the rancho de las Calabasas are the ruins of an old church with the altar still standing and the bell hanging in the belfry. The road from Tucson lay in the valley of the Santa Cruz as far as this ranch which is occupied by two Germans. A third brother has been killed by the Indians and all their cattle and horses have been stolen by the savages. The two brothers kept an awful old 'bachelor hall'."

Plenty of water for irrigation on good soil brought Indians and Mexicans back to occupy Calabasas during what proved to be only a short lull between Apache raids. Late in 1854 engineer Peter Bady, surveying the 32nd parallel for a rail line, was camped on the Sonoita when he was informed by two Mexicans recently escaped from Apache warriors that their captors were planning to attack Calabasas again and this time kill everybody. Bady took ten men and headed for the

town, meeting on the way sixty Mexican dragoons and forty Apache *mansos* (tamed or domesticated Apaches) who joined his party. Reaching the ranch, now headed by Don Frederico Hulseman, Bady made known the impending danger and instructed Hulseman to his plan, retreating with his forces to heavy brush cover a few hundred yards from the ranch.

About mid-day the watching Hulseman spotted advancing Apaches and blew a high-pitched call on the cavalry bugle as prearranged. Bady and men responded at once, mounting and charging directly into the center of the two hundred Apaches. He later reported, "No cry of mercy was given and no mercy shown." Most of the invaders were killed outright by the Mexican dragoons, the wounded finished off by the mansos, leaving not one survivor. Not long after the slaughter Bady received a dinner invitation from Don Frederico. "Before we eat," the host said, "let me show you something." What Bady saw in the courtyard was the three-foot string of dried Apache ears.

Some protection was being extended by U.S. troops, the territory having become part of the United States the year before. In 1861 the soldiers were removed to fight in the Civil War and the town of the pumpkins was again left to the mercy of the Apaches. In 1864 peripatetic reporter J. Ross Browne wrote to his magazine, Harper's, that he

MOUNT WRIGHTSON, FROM CALABAZA, SANTA CRUZ VALLEY.

PLAN OF THE HOTEL AND PLAZA AT CALABASAS AS IT WILL APPEAR WHEN COMPLETED

had visited the valley, a place of rich soil, ample irrigation and surrounded by mines of copper and gold. "It might be made profitable in the hands of some enterprising American . . . at present, however, military protection in the country is worthless owing to the incursion of the Apaches." He recounted the well known story of Mrs. Page, daughter of early settler "Old Man" Pennington, of how she was captured, tortured and thrown into a gulch for dead, and how after several days of near unconsciousness she managed to crawl to a point where she was seen and rescued.

By 1878 nearby Tucson was in the throes of a boom, fast building up with stores and saloons for travelers arriving at the Old Pueblo. At this time two men from San Francisco chose Calabasas as a delightful place for a luxury hotel. They were John H. Curry, ex-judge, and Charles P. Sykes, newspaper publisher, both visionaries. They went to ex-Gov. Gandra and brother-in-law Aguilar and from them purchased the site for about $6,000.

In late 1878 Tucson papers noted there was much activity at the old town, that the whole area was being surveyed and a hotel building started. Col. Sykes was quoted as saying his hotel would be two-storied and made of brick being fired in the vicinity as the stables and corral would also be. G. W. Atkinson, the best brick man in San Francisco had been hired to oversee the project. Sykes sent out glittering brochures and worked up much enthusiasm for his new hotel. On the negative side the Tombstone *Epitaph* sneered at what it called "Pumpkinville," fully expecting Sykes to

have heavy ocean going vessels plying the Santa Cruz right to the town, unloading world merchandise at its teeming docks.

Yet in spite of these and other spoofing attitudes with dire warnings that the Apaches would stop the building, the hotel was finished. In October of 1882 Sykes arranged for a large delegation from Tucson to come to Calabasas for the grand opening, hiring the Tucson Brass Band to serenade the party all the way. The group left Tucson at 5 a.m. and finally arrived in Calabasas dog-tired in the evening, the account adding, "as only water was available to drink along the way."

Col. Sykes welcomed the party with open arms and uncorked bottles. He fed the delegates roasts of mutton, chicken, beef and game, including wild turkey, quail, plover and British snipe. After supper the party observed floors covered with Brussels carpet, solid black walnut furniture in every room. Plied with more spirits the party danced until midnight. Sightseeing the next day, all returned to Tucson singing praise for Sykes' hotel, "the best between San Francisco and Denver."

Not long after the successful grand opening the colonel began to miss some of his cattle and after several more depredations the losses were traced to the Apaches. One night they were so bold as to enter the brick corral and drag away a pair of blooded black carriage horses. Probably unable to ride them the savages killed the blacks not far from the hotel. Next they kidnaped three members of the Peck family in the area and brutally murdered them. In spite of all this Col. Sykes carried on, filling his registers with the names of some of the most prominent people in the country.

But the end of the dream was coming up sharply. In 1894 the Court of Private Land Claims voided all Spanish land grants along the border. The action wiped out Boston syndicates operating mines leased from Col. Sykes, townsite of Calabasas and hotel. Sykes died on a trip to New York City, his widow living in a room in the hotel until her death in 1910 and the heirs made their homes in houses near it, using some rooms for hay storage after the mother passed away. In 1927 fire broke out in the stored fodder and the entire building burned to the ground, bricks and other unburnables hauled away by Indians and ranchers. Calabasas, distilled from blood and courage, is today almost invisible.

PUZZLING ARRANGEMENT of wooden posts few feet from adobe ruin at edge of Calabasas cotton field. Framed is what appears to be same peak called Mount Wrightson in old sketch. Named for Prof. W. Wrightson, early historian, peak often called Old Baldy now, is highest in Santa Cruz County. One of author's few clues in locating Calabasas was lining up peak as in old drawing of town.

ONE MAN REGIMENT

Pete Kitchen Ranch, Arizona

The Apaches came down "like wolves on the fold" and Arizona ranchers felt the bitter sting of defeat and death. But not Pete Kitchen. He said his hogs looked like walking pincushions with all the arrows sticking out of them and he saw to it they did not stick out of him. "So many men lost their lives in the neighborhood," said Thomas Casanega, who married one of Kitchen's nieces, "if all their bodies were laid side by side like railroad ties they would make a track from Nogales to Potero."

Pete Kitchen was the very essence of stubborn resistance. Although under almost constant attack by Apaches he stood his ground among ranchers who gave up the struggle. The few settlers courageous enough to hold out for a time said of him, "To the Apache he was more terrible than an army with banners."

Frank Rockwood in his book *Arizona Characters* says Pete Kitchen was the connecting link between savagery and civilization. Kitchen left some memoirs showing how clear is this delineation of the man's make-up. He kept much fine stock at his farm near the Mexican border, the fat animals a constant temptation to early cattle rustlers. When

HOME of self-sufficient rancher Pete Kitchen. One of the oldest in Arizona, adobe building was set up in 1850s. It stands several hundred feet from rancher's "fortress" and just left, out of photo, is private cemetery for unknown number of men who dared attack doughty pioneer.

he missed one of his favorite horses and found well-marked tracks pointed toward the border, the outraged rancher got on another good steed and set out after the thief. "I caught up with him some distance south of the line," he wrote, "and put my gun on him, making him return with me. After tying the man to a tree branch overhead with a rope around his neck, I laid down to rest. When I woke up the horse he had been sitting on had wandered some little distance, and much to my surprise, the rope around his neck had strangled him."

Although savage natives killed most of his neighbors, tortured and murdered his favorite herder and slaughtered his stepson, Kitchen fought on. In time the Apaches got the message and left him in comparative peace. He gave all victims of carnage on his ranch decent burial in a private "Boot Hill" near his little adobe ranch home. Not knowing who most were, he did not identify the graves but wife Dona Rose, a deeply devout Catholic, religiously burned candles for them in hope of salvation for their souls.

PETE KITCHEN FORTRESS on rocky knoll with view of fields. Contemporary wrote, "There is a sentinel posted on the roof, there is another out in the cienaga with the stock. The men plowing the bottoms are obliged to carry rifles cocked and swung to the plow handle. Every man and boy, and indeed the women, had to go armed. At the fort there are rifles, revolvers and shotguns along the walls and in every corner. Everything speaks of warfare and bloodshed."
When photo was made in 1964 building housed museum operated by owner Col. Gilbert Proctor who kindly allowed author to camp beside it. Historic structure is now operated by Henry Molina family as one of several Casa Molina restaurants in area. Mundane use seems almost sacrilege but occupation of any sort almost guarantees preservation, abandonment leading to swift decay.

OLD RAILROAD CAR abandoned among much other rail equipment, mining machinery. Artifacts at Twin Buttes cannot be approached too closely, all sections behind fences. Photo made by special permission. Cactus plant is Opuntia species, this one with slabs of brilliant cerise-purple.

GHOST BEHIND BARBED WIRE

Twin Buttes, Arizona

Copper mining began in what was locally called the Borracho Mines some time in the early 1870s. Located in the mountains 26 miles southwest of Tucson, Arizona, miners named the town that developed Twin Buttes for a pair of nearby peaks. Mining there was sporadic for the first three decades, as little money was available to small-time Mexican operators and digging was done mostly by pick and shovel methods. When the copper veins thickened, activity increased until the deposit pinched out. Then everybody indulged in a siesta.

Near the turn of the century "The Three Nations" began wide-scale operations in the mines. American John G. Baxter, Irish Michael Irish and Scotch John Ellis, seeing what they called "an inexhaustible

supply" of copper ore, began by prospecting both old and new workings. Results were so encouraging and news releases so enthusiastic that a group of Milwaukee financiers bought out the whole thing, incorporating the Twin Buttes Mining and Smelting Co. with assets of $1,000,000 under the laws of Arizona Territory. Before incorporation was fully accomplished, the new company's prospectors made a happy discovery. The Morgan Mine had an ore body 95 feet deep, 25 feet wide and 300 feet long, with ore assaying 10%.

That same year, the company made plans to build a 500-ton smelter and construct a railroad from Tucson to the now roaring copper camp. The railroad would supplant transport by wagon and team and the new smelter would handle the huge amounts of ore pouring from the Morgan Mine and that royal trio, the Copper King, Copper Queen and Copper Prince.

By this time, Twin Buttes had acquired a newspaper, but it wasn't printed in town and it wasn't intended for local consumption. The *Twin Buttes Times*, edited and printed in Milwaukee, was aimed at stockholders. Bubbling with enthusiasm and carrying the Twin Buttes dateline for authenticity, it delivered the glad news that not only would the new railroad carry ores and supplies for Twin Buttes itself, but already applications were being received from other mining districts with requests for spurs. Among these, the *Times* said, were the Helvetia Mines in the Santa Ritas and the Lincoln Mining Company, which consisted of 31 claims in the Sierrita Mountains. The paper continuously stressed forthcoming benefits of the railroad because under territorial law, the Twin Buttes Mining and Smelting Company had to establish a second corporation, The Twin Buttes Railroad, in order to build the railroad. So stockholders, traditionally

OCOTILLO, technically Fourqueieria splendens is widespread throughout warmer sections of southern deserts. This one near Patagonia is in full display of scarlet bloom. Plant is not related to cactus tribe, has own method of coping with scant or non-existent moisture. In rain, regardless of season, shrub puts forth leaves, flowers. Here foliage has dropped to be replaced by bloom.

dazzled by an aura of rich paying mines, had to be infected by railroad fever, too.

Contrary to dire predictions, the projected railroad was actually built. The new Twin Buttes Railroad, connecting with the Southern Pacific in Tucson, ran in a southerly direction through Santa Clara Valley to Sahuarita. Then, swinging westerly in easy grades and curves, it ascended to Twin Buttes. Shortly after leaving Tucson, travelers on the railroad were treated to a close-up view of Mission San Xavier, that dazzling "White Dove of the Desert." The railroad advertised that it was prepared to accept general freight such as hardware, machinery, milk, cream and meat, the latter three items, it was stressed, at "shipper's risk." For the first few years, the railroad was a huge success. Twin Buttes Mines shipped large quantities of ore of types not handled at the local smelters, freight and passenger business was good, and some of the spur extensions were actually constructed.

Then, around 1907, the line unaccountably laid off employees and some freight shipments were "lost." Dissatisfied customers complained of poor service and high rates. In a few months both mine and railroad companies were overdrawn at the bank. About this time, a Twin Buttes Mining and Smelter stock offer was made of 250,000 shares at 60 cents, the offer almost immediately moderated to 40 cents. There were few takers. Bad times had hit Twin Buttes.

By 1910, the original company was pretty much disbanded. John Ellis, one of the "Three Nation" men who had gone along with the Twin Butte setup, married in Tempe, then returned to Scotland, where he died in 1909. Michael Irish married in Tucson, then took his new bride and copper wealth to the old country. But the other member, John C. Baxter, stepped in when the company closed down operation of the Twin Buttes properties and together with Ed Bush, reopened the Morgan. The start of World War I gave their new company a big boost and the railroad once again carried a car of ore every week. This boom was temporary, however. After the war, things again declined at the Buttes.

As deposits grew thinner, general economic conditions grew steadily worse and soon Twin Buttes became a ghost town. The railroad also faded into a shadowy spectre. Of the town, little is left, and this unreachable behind barbed wire. (Reprinted by courtesy of *Desert Magazine*.)

MOST OLD ADOBE BUILDINGS in Patagonia retain plaster coating that conceals original construction and age. Town at north end of gravel road connecting Arizona State 82 with Mexican border was named by early Spanish explorers for "big footed Indians", and is taking off point for number of fascinating, little known ghost mining camps. Century ago, shortly after U.S. acquired area from Mexico in Gadsden Purchase 359 mining claims existed within 15 mile radius of Patagonia. Most recently operated mines in vicinity were those of American Smelter and Mining Co. which closed down in November of 1957. Town still has fair population but nothing like formerly when mines operated.

ROAD SIDE SHRINE just south of Patagonia on State 82 reached by short climb up steep steps. Southern Arizona has many such, some conveniently beside the highway. They serve devout Catholics as something like second church where prayers, devotions may be said.

DETAIL of roadside shrine near Patagonia.

TWO-YEAR BOOM TOWN

Harshaw, Arizona

The Harshaw mining camp in southern Arizona was built on a solid silver foundation in the center of the Patagonia Mountains. Midway between two main river valleys, it lay athwart the path of history, each movement of people passing that way leaving its mark. Indians living along Sobaioura Creek called the area "Enchanted Land" because of streams flowing generously with clear water which provided an ample growth of good grass. Spaniards came later but stayed only long enough to call those Indians "Patagonias" for their reputed large feet.

The padres who arrived next considered all of Primeria Alta a fertile field for conversion, creating devils for the Indians to labor against for more than three hundred years. Then Spain relinquished the country to the Republic of Mexico which put the padres out and their adobe structures untended, to melt away and leave only peach orchards here and there. Mexican families settling in the narrow canyon where the boom town of Harshaw would spring up, found some of the gnarled trees and named their village Durazno for "place of the peaches." With the Gadsden Purchase which made the Patagonias part of the United States came "yankees" with pick and shovel, including David Tecumseh Harshaw.

One of the stalwarts who left comfortable homes in the east to hunt for gold in California, Harshaw was born in New York in 1828 and just 20 when he traveled overland to work in Nevada County mines, probably at Grass Valley. At the outbreak of the Civil War he joined First California Volunteer Infantry mustered at Oakland and was promptly sent to Tucson.

After the war Harshaw traveled around looking for a good place to raise cattle, finally settling in the San Pedro Valley of southern Arizona with about 1000 head. On these forage lands the young veteran found good deposits of gold and silver, in the Santa Ritas, not far south of Tucson. Nell Murbarger in her definitive *Ghosts of the Adobe Walls*, classic of Arizona's mining days, gives reports from the Tucson *Arizona Citizen* in 1875, that "David T. Harshaw brought in a sack of dust and

nuggets weighing $843, the result of four days' labor for three men . . . the Santa Rita placers are entitled to rank equal with the best placers ever discovered."

Perhaps Harshaw's claim petered out, possibly he was run off by Indians, but one thing for sure, he was running cattle on lands properly allocated for use by Chiricahua Apaches. When they complained to Indian Agent Thomas J. Jeffords the official summarily ordered Harshaw to take his cattle and decamp. Forthwith he drove the animals to a section of the Patagonia Mountains not far south of the town of that name. With plenty of grass and water Harshaw felt he had greatly improved his position, especially when he could get supplies at the Mexican village of Durazno. Again he found metal, his first claims the Hardshell and Harshaw, just south of Durazno which he worked only long enough to prove their potential worth and then sold both in 1879. Having bequeathed his name on the one-time Mexican village he married Maria Jesus Andrada, sister of his partner Jose, and settled down to operate a stage station at Davidson's Springs where he died in September

NEGLECTED GRAVE in one of the two cemeteries at edge of Harshaw, marker not stating and War Dept. unable to determine cause of soldier's death in mining camp. Only one cemetery here is contemporary with Harshaw's brief period of prosperity, 1879-81. Some tombstones are still in evidence, though almost covered by brush, weeds. Cattle around, drop manure on graves of pioneers.

of 1884. His obituary said, "David Harshaw was a typical frontiersman, a man with a big heart, the very essence of noble qualities."

And his name was used with electric excitement when that same year the Southern Pacific entered Tucson and a boisterous boom began at Harshaw nee Durazno. In 1880 James Reilly, editor of *Territorial Expositor* of Phoenix, described it as easily the biggest camp he had ever seen outside of Tombstone. That same year managers of the mines arrived with much needed eastern capital to open a large scale development, their chief investment being in the mine located by David Harshaw, consisting of three parallel ledges from 5 feet to 25 feet wide. A gang of men was hired to grade off a section of steep hillside for installation of a new reduction mill scheduled to arrive in due time by railroad to Tucson.

Within six months the 20-stamp Hermosa Mill was crushing 75 tons of ore every day, making it the largest producer in Arizona. Editor Reilly now wrote that any attempt to evaluate potential wealth of the Harshaw properties would be "preposterous." Silver was soon pouring out to the tune of $365,000 every month. 600 people had arrived to share in the boom, most of them adventurers from 35 states and 3 territories according to the Census Schedule of Arizona Territory of 1880. China, India and Mexico were also represented, several dozen from Ireland.

Only 100 men listed themselves as miners. 24 called themselves grocers, the same number liquor sellers. Restaurants employed 35, laundries 11, the others accounted for in such businesses as livery stables, blacksmith shops, wagonmakers, freighters, barber shops. A few candid individuals listed their calling as faro bank dealers and speculators. There was a "bell hanger," whatever occupation that was. Those were male registrants and as for the 64 females, only two kinds of work were given. Most of them were housewives, 4 forthrightly calling themselves prostitutes. Mexican women predominated, most of them mothers with 59 young children. The Harshaw population was youthful, Mike Fagan, large and powerful ex-peace officer, was the oldest man in town at 45.

A newspaper was started, several hotels and as one Tucson reporter wrote it, "every other establishment in town a saloon." Harshaw was undeniably a real city but this status lasted little more than two years, for two reasons. Silver veins grew thin, then pinched out to almost nothing. The largest mine, the Hermosa, which employed 200 men, closed down, retaining only a skeleton force to guard property and make small exploratory borings for the vanished silver vein. The second disaster was a flood caused by cloudbursts in the Patagonias which poured a huge wall of water down the one street in the narrow canyon. A muddy, boulder-carrying deluge tore out all but the more sturdy stone structures, some of them standing today. The ones destroyed were rebuilt with lumber but a bad fire consumed them, the stone buildings again spared. This gave little incentive to rebuilding and Harshaw died as a town.

The *Arizona Weekly Citizen* of July 7, 1888, reported, "A few of the buildings are still standing in a good state of preservation, though unoccupied for several years. . . . About nine families now live in Harshaw." As of today a census would show about the same population, most of the people Spanish-speaking Mexicans (see Boot Hill).

CATHOLIC CHURCH, one of Harshaw's solidly built stone edifices, commented upon by newspapers of Tucson and other cities. Escaping flood and withstanding less dramatic ravages of time, stone walls are being exposed by cracking plaster coating.

SCENE IN OLD CEMETERY of original village of Durazno. Though most graves are very old, metal markers shown here indicate more recent burials of Mexican townsfolk. Gnarled mesquite tree overhangs graves, on it suspended several wire rings, foundations for wreaths of paper flowers.

PLACID BURROS wander at will along Harshaw's one street.

HOW HE WON THE BATTLE AND LOST THE WAR

Mowry, Arizona

It was certainly a duel in the sun and it might have been one to the death. For there was a challenge in the true spirit and tradition of gallantry. It was accepted and seconds appointed. The duelists met and the former lieutenant fired. But it was not a very good rifle and he was not a very good shot and his antagonist was not a very serious enemy. So instead of killing him he went over and shook his hand.

Dramatic discoveries of silver in the Patagonia Mountains in 1736 brought a crowd of treasure seekers and caused King Philip V of Spain to claim the area as his own. According to persistent rumors the mines at Mowry were originally worked by Jesuit priests. If so their efforts were forgotten but still evident when a pair of Mexicans came along about 1857.

These men from south of the border (16 miles away) were sharp enough to discover that working a silver mine was not as easy as panning for gold, that it would require capital and machinery far beyond their means. They sold out at the first offer, from officers stationed at nearby Fort Crittenden. The Americans found the same problems, that they had no cornucopia that would effortlessly pour forth riches in gleaming silver. And when they saw they could not work together they gladly accepted the bid from Lt. Sylvester Mowry, also at the fort.

DANCE HALL, one of best preserved structures in extensive town growing up around Sylvester Mowry's extremely rich silver-lead mines, only metropolitan center in area. It had hotels, saloons, gambling places, stores, almost all built of adobe. When this photo was made in 1963 buildings were good enough to merit listing as "complete town for sale" in Tubac real estate office. By 1967 porch had collapsed, more plaster fallen, but still structurally solid. Tree is one most characteristic of area—interior live oak (as distinguished from California coastal tree). Live oak has evergreen, holly-like leaves, small acorns.

Mowry resigned from the army and devoted his energies to the mine. One of his problems was the roads were little more than trails and there would be no railroad for many years. With a crew of Mexican peons he started deepening the shafts and tunnels and before long his men were ascending ladders with astoundingly rich loads of silver-lead ore. This looked like success and he renamed the Patagonia mine for himself. As the Mowry it would produce over $1 million in one three-year period.

Galena was the ore, at first roughly refined in Mexican blast furnaces at Lochiel on the border, the lead and silver bars weighing about 70 pounds, shipped to Europe and sold in England for $200 per ton. But shortly pure silver was being cast locally into bars worth from $200 to $300 and used as a medium of exchange in an area still lacking in currency.

With the fantastic success of his mines making headlines in Eastern and European press, Mowry received many offers to speak in public at good fees. He turned the management of the mine over to several good men and went on what amounted to a chautauqua circuit. In one speech he declared that all streams in Arizona teemed with fish. However the eastern audience evaluated the overstatement, one Edward Cross of Tubac, Arizona, correspondent of the St. Louis *Republican*, bristled indignantly. In printed comment he ridiculed Mowry's brash utterance, saying he had found a few fish as long as his fingernail, that these must be the "Mowry trout."

Stung by the article, Mowry surprised Cross by demanding satisfaction in a formal duel. Reluctant but game, Cross met his challenger near Tubac (an old town near the Mission Tumacacori). The affair was widely publicized and attended by a gallery largely from Tucson, gamblers from mining camps having a field day placing bets.

Chosen as weapons were Burnside rifles and neither mine owner nor newsman knew much about using them. The first three shots went wild

COMPANY OFFICE interior, deteriorating but for Civil War vintage, still in good condition. Picture taken in 1963 shows usual adobe and plaster construction, streaks on wall seen thru door at left made by water leaking from roof.

MAIN GUARD TOWER overlooking Yuma Territorial Penitentiary. Gatling gun here frustrated most escapes. Water was pumped to tank under platform. During Civil War Sylvester Mowry was confined in this notorious prison, charged with treason, Union government maintaining mine owner provided lead bullets to Confederates. (For story and other photos of prison see **Tales the Western Tombstones Tell.**)

all his energies to them he might have made it through the war but there was talk about his sympathies being with the Confederate forces. A Rhode Islander by birth with no record of antipathy toward the Union cause, his continued public utterances were somehow construed as treachery to the North.

On June 8, 1862, Sylvester Mowry was arrested for treason. Gen. Carlton ordered the accused made prisoner on charges that Mowry had rendered aid and comfort to the enemy by producing for Confederate armies bullets manufactured of lead from his mines. The Union government seized them and confiscated all silver and lead produced.

The prisoner was immediately taken to Yuma and thrown into its notorious, dreaded territorial prison, it being reported he was "closely confined" which indicated incarceration in the "Hell Hole" or dungeon. There he languished until November when he was suddenly released and informed there was not a shred of evidence against him. In spite of complete exoneration Mowry found himself destitute, with no hope of any property being restored to him.

He brought suit against Gen. Carlton and the government for $1 million but all efforts to collect were frustrated especially after the mines were sold at public auction for $4,000. Some historians claim he was paid damages but others dispute this. Most agree Mowry went to London, England, where he died in poverty in 1871.

and then Mowry's gun failed to discharge. The seconds agreed he was entitled to another try but as he raised the weapon he saw Cross with arms folded, bravely ready for the bullet. Firing the rifle into the air, Mowry walked over to Cross and extended his hand. Both declared themselves satisfied, and later both made public retractions of their bitter statements.

Mowry's mines were producing $1,000 a day when the Civil War broke out. Had he devoted

CENTRALLY LOCATED building assumed to be mine company office, photo taken in 1963. Roads wind thru town as main street, visitor continuing along good surface about 1 mile, taking left fork up hill, exploring manzanita brush at left, will bring him to cemetery. Just back of point from which photo was taken is fork leading sharply left and steeply up nearer hill. About ¾ mile up slope are located big Mowry mines and small village dating from World War I days, now as deserted as main town.

OLD MOWRY CEMETERY is hard to find, author forced to unravel complicated directions in Spanish given by nearest human, elderly Mexican woman living near Harshaw. Graveyard is "Boot Hill" in true popular meaning. Markers are gone but history records 17 white men buried here. 15 dying by violence.

Two were J. B. Mills and Edward Stevens, visiting at San Antonio mine across nearby Mexican border. Ambushed by Indians they were strung up by heels to limb of oak tree, savages burning slow fires under heads of still living victims. Bodies were found later by comrades and buried here.

Not long after tragedy a Dr. Titus and accompanying Delaware Indian were attacked at same place, Indian killed at once. Titus got off horse, clawed up hill thru thorny brush 200 yards, then shot in hip. Choosing death to inevitable torture, he killed himself, was later found and buried here.

OFFICE BUILDING photographed in June, 1967, showing grievous deterioration in 4 years (compare with accompanying photo made in Nov. 1963). Mowry is among author's favorite ghost towns, saddening decay observed in course of many visits. Roof has collapsed allowing rain to wash away walls of unbaked adobe bricks. Note comparatively good condition of wall sections still protected by roof.

FEW BUILDINGS in Mowry were constructed of lumber, this one only partially so. Metal roofs generally seen were likely placed during temporary boom in World War I years. Leafless saplings in this Nov. view are young "Trees of Heaven", originally introduced by Chinese.

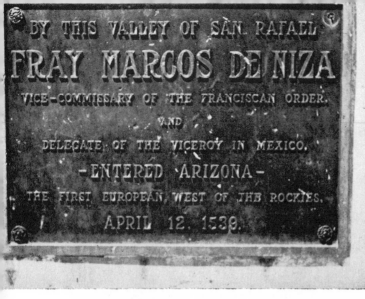

DETAIL OF PLAQUE on monument to de Niza on international border. Early explorer was Italian in service of Spain, sent early in 1539 from Mexico City to northern country. He was under orders of Antonio de Mendoza to find fabled Seven Cities of Cibola, rumored to have streets paved with solid gold. De Niza was accompanied by legendary Negro slave Estevan who awed Indians with gaudy attire, feathers, bells. Sent ahead, Estevan reached site near present Gallup, N.M., and attempting to use status to seduce Zuni girls, was killed by braves.

IMPRESSIVE MONUMENT to Fra Marcos de Niza stands just north of U.S.-Mexico boundary at Lochiel. Border crossing here is permitted for short periods only in morning and afternoon. Neither town nor highway on Mexican side. Blooming plants are "desert poppies" or argemones.

ADOBE BUILDING, one of few remaining in Lochiel. With sheet metal roof recently blown off, it is doomed to early dissolution by rain, which though rare comes in heavy down pours. Tiny hamlet on border has long been scene of smuggling activities, of many battles between Mexicans, Indians.

In 1858 small Mexican girl, Inez Gonzales, was abducted. Her uncle and large military escort were sent to rescue her, uncle and most of escort killed in fight over her. Later Boundary Commissioner John R. Bartlett was successful in negotiations, regaining her, seeing she was returned to parents in Santa Cruz, Mex. Last industry at border town was primitive Mexican type smelter used to refine first silver ores from Mowry mine just north in U.S.

The plaque reads:

BY THIS VALLEY OF SAN RAFAEL
FRAY MARCOS DE NIZA
VICE-COMMISSARY OF THE FRANCISCAN ORDER,
AND
DELEGATE OF THE VICEROY IN MEXICO,
—ENTERED ARIZONA—
THE FIRST EUROPEAN WEST OF THE ROCKIES,
APRIL 12, 1539.

SUBSTANTIAL ADOBE BUILDING in Washington was still occupied when author first visited in 1963 but deserted on later occasions. Town had population of 1,000 in heyday. In 1967 only one house was inhabited, this at opposite end of town, across gulch. Similarly good-sized store on main street was in operation in 1963, later closed.

WASHINGTON, often referred to as Washington Camp, just north of Duquesne with which its history is closely linked. Shown here is barn-residence at Washington where all remaining structures are of adobe in contrast to sister city with mostly frame relics. Novelty in area of silver-lead mines, as in nearby Mowry, was Pride of the West, producing wealth of copper under ownership of historically prominent Sen. W. A. Clark of Montana and Jerome X. Mineis. Million and a half was said to have been rolled out in 8 years.

HEAD-FRAME of large Bonanza Mine at Duquesne. Either copper or lead-silver was produced here, dumps (now posted) displaying much blue-green rock strongly resembling copper ore.
There is legend that George Westinghouse lived and mined here. Truth seems to be that while he may have visited he did not live here, no biographies including such information. However Westinghouse interests in Pittsburgh, Pa. did mine here, naming camp Duquesne after Fort Duquesne, erected by French forces in 1754, site later became city of Pittsburgh.

COPPER IN APACHELAND

Dos Cabezas, Arizona

The old town of Dos Cabezas lies sleeping in an easy hollow between two low mountain ranges. Conspicuous on the summit of one and directly above the near-deserted camp are the twin granite knobs that give the town and range the name, Dos Cabezas, Spanish for "Two Heads." Hardy Spanish explorers named it as they did many noticeable landmarks in the early 1500s when they scoured the southwest seeking the fabled Seven Cities of Cibola.

Later Mexicans forced the native Chiricahua

Apaches from the area and after the end of the war with Mexico and acquisition through the Gadsden Purchase, the country was opened up to white settlers. The first party to camp at Dos Cabezas Spring was composed of soldiers under command of the Capt. Richard Stoddard Elwell who became a Confederate officer of some note. He found the spring of good water directly on the emigrant trail, originally an Indian trail, and camped there before the Gadsden Act was ratified. Later he returned to establish the first stage station in the area, a building erected close to

ADOBE STRUCTURE reputed to be Butterfield Stage Station, built in 1858. It was erected as overnight stop for Argonauts heading for California gold fields. John Butterfield chose location nearer center of town than near Elwell's Spring where community started. First building there was long used as family residence. After some years residents fled house in terror, saying ghosts chased them away. Another family moved in with same results. The whiteclad spirits were reported hovering near and making unearthly noises. At last historic building was razed, a sacrifice to superstition. This second stage station will soon crumble away, stone foundation prolonging survival.

DOS CABEZAS STORE was spared general destruction for unexplained reason when town died as important mining center. Large company dance hall, center of joy unconfined for 20 years, remains as shell at left. Each house in town had own well, this old one with concrete curbing. Shaft now serves as daytime home for large horned owl who sleeps on rocky ledge, shows strong resentment at being disturbed by snapping bill.

Elwell's Spring of gushing water. Some of the tired emigrants stopped at this sign of civilization and refused to go on.

They were easy prey for the Apaches who pillaged and plundered in a reign of terror that whites seemed as unable to repel as Mexicans had earlier. At the end of eighteen months, sixteen stages and drivers failed to get to the Spring, almost certainly having fallen victims to the savages. The burned remains of one stage was located nearby, the nude body of one man bearing more than a hundred inch-deep burns made by fire brands. The station then closed down. Several others attempted to operate it, Jim Birch being one who held off the Indians until 1858. Then came John Butterfield who made stage coach history. Precious metals were being worked near Cabezas and in 1858 he located his new stage stop a quarter mile from the old spring site, nearer the nucleus of what was rapidly becoming a town.

By this time Dos Cabezas was a center for prospectors, some of them just passing through, others finding traces of metal in the nearby hills. Several small mines were operating and "home made" mills established. With Elwell's Spring no longer adequate for the increased population and too far from the new "city center", a well was dug which proved to be a large success, the water table showing at shallow depths. Every family had a handy supply of water in the back yard, each well equipped with a hand windlass and wooden bucket at the end of a rope.

About 1906 a man known only as "Old Man Mitchell" ran across a rich vein of copper just north of town near the foot of the range. The simple prospector had neither strength nor money to develop his claim, but talk about it reached another man who though also lacking money, had initiative. T. N. McCauley bought the property and then searched out wealthy, influential men

WRECKED ADOBES line main street of old mining town. Dos Cabezas Range makes backdrop but displays only one "head" from this point.

who organized the Mascot Copper Company, Inc.

The new company installed the most modern equipment at the mine and built a modern complex near it to house officials and personnel. Dormitories for store employees flanked a movie house, grade school, cafeteria, store, dairy and numerous other facilities. A generator supplied electricity. All structures utilized the easily obtainable adobe and were plastered neatly white. Mexican laborers did the work being familiar with adobe construction. Although development of housing had gone on at top speed, adobe took time and all manner of tents and shacks went up to temporary use of mine and office workers and their families.

For twenty years the Mascot was big news in mining journals. The company built a smelter that cost many thousands, a new powerhouse about a million. Irked at having to haul copper to the nearest railhead at Wilcox, Mascot built its own railroad to that point.

For a time the town had its own post office. Its biggest business was sorting out the daily mail orders with money and checks for stock, and mailing out gilt-edged certificates. Then this stopped abruptly for shortly after the big powerhouse was finished miners came up to daylight with bad news. The rich lode of copper had come to an end. Experts were sent into the mine to survey the situation and they could find no metal, so at a time when prosperity and optimism were at their heights, copper mining at Dos Cabezas was something in the past.

More than 300 employees were told there would be no more checks and to leave town if they could. Those owning the little frame houses sold them for pittances. Wrecking balls were swung against all permanent-type buildings including offices, dormitories and the showplace powerhouse. Dos Cabezas became an instant ghost town.

Several families stll make the town of two heads their home, living there in the hope that some day another copper vein may be uncovered or having nowhere else to go. Nell Merwin is one who likes the town and clings stubbornly to her old home, one of the oldest houses still standing, a museum of relics and artifacts of old Dos Cabezas. She likes people, the town that was and takes pride in entertaining random visitors interested in the history of the one time copper metropolis. She provided most of this story of Dos Cabezas.

PROMINENT DOUBLE PEAK named Dos Cabezas by Spanish explorers searching for fabled Seven Cities of Cibola with streets of gold who passed this way in early 1500s. Cacti in foreground is wickedly vicious "Jumping Cholla" reputedly leaping at man on horseback, attacking with spines. Fable is near truth, joints breaking off at slightest touch, each spine bearing recurved barbs for better digging.

New Mexico

TURQUOISE TOWN

Cerrillos, New Mexico

No one can say just when Cerrillos (properly Los Cerrillos, "the little hills") had its beginning. Certainly the diggings there are very ancient, gold and turquoise mined in the low mountains around the town since at least 500 A.D. when Basket Maker Indians were in their prime. A few miles from Mt. Chalchihuitl is a huge pit in the solid rock and across Galisteo Creek and up a winding arroyo is the famed Mina del Tiro, "Mine of the Shaft." All evidence is that prehistoric Indians were the miners. History comes into somewhat sharper focus with the likelihood that those gold and silver ores assayed by Spanish prospector Espejo in 1582 came from the Little Hills.

Indian revolutionist Po-pe led his tribesmen against the hated Spanish in 1680, driving those not murdered out of the country. Setting up new quarters at El Paso del Norte Spanish fugitives forgot all about mining or at least made no further attempts to regain the turquoise and gold at Los Cerrillos, all locations being lost.

Three hundred years after Espejo, in 1879, prospecting Americans rediscovered precious metals and blue turquoise at Los Cerrillos and the ancient diggings. A rush followed with more than three hundred men swarming over the little hills. Not long after this the Santa Fe Railroad came through, setting off an even larger boom, satellite towns like Bonanza and Carbonateville mushrooming briefly. It was during this heated period that eastern capital came in to reopen the old turquoise mines, the two largest being the Tiffany and Castilian. An 1899 report listed New Mexico's production of turquoise as worth $1,600,000, most of it coming from Cerrillos, Yankees having dropped the "Los."

With production of metals and blue gemstones lessening, the town began to fail after the turn of the century. There was some activity as long as neighboring Madrid flourished. When tipples there ceased to load coal cars and the railroad curtailed operations, something in Cerrillos died too. It has withered since although a tavern still serves an occasional thirsty rancher or tourist, a general store and restaurant open part time.

OLDEST BUILDING remaining in Cerrillos, it is presumed. Pine logs from mountains were squared with broad axe, laid up with minimum notching, wide chinks filled with mud. Portion at far left received coat of elegant plaster in later years.

HE BROUGHT LIGHT IN

Madrid, N.M.

Nobody thought a nice fellow like Lloyd, clerk at the Albuquerque and Cerrillos Coal Co., would ever be put in jail . . . and there was the sheriff going to the Cerrillos railroad station after somebody else. Well after all, this was Madrid, New Mexico, where anything might happen. It did, that night. They let Lloyd out of jail on the promise of a keg of beer, the sheriff brought Marjorie in and the miners threw a big party for the bride and groom.

Coal was found at Madrid as early as 1839 and probably used at the nearby Cerrillos gold mines. When Gen. Stephen Watts Kearney came through New Mexico in the 1840s he used Madrid coal for his army. And it is said that at one time ox teams hauled the coal all the way to St. Louis.

Legends grow more factual when the Madrid mines were opened by a subsidary of the Santa Fe Railway in the early 1880s. In 1899 when the town had a population of 3,000 the Colorado Fuel and Iron Co. took control, later selling to the Albuquerque and Cerrillos Coal Co. In 1910 Oscar Huber went to work for the company, eventually buying them out, the property still owned by his heirs in 1964.

Marjorie Lloyd came to the coal camp as a bride in 1913, she recalled in a *New Mexico Magazine* article. Her new husband was very much concerned about the charivari that might greet them when they arrived from Denver as bride and groom. He was employed in the camp as mine clerk and well aware of rowdy welcomes of the sort. He arranged to have the Madrid sheriff meet their train in Cerrillos, three miles distant, and spirit them into his home unobserved.

The miners however discovered why the clerk went to Denver and the next day through a ruse managed to lock him up in the town jail. Kept a prisoner until dinner time, Lloyd was glad to buy his freedom with a keg of beer and the traditional charivari was staged after all.

At that time, as now, the residential district consisted of four long, dreary rows of houses sadly in need of paint. They faced the company store, offices, tavern and other business, a row of shade trees bordering both sides of the main street. The population was about 3,000 and there were no vacant homes, the Lloyds being forced to live at one of the three boarding houses, the one having the only green lawn in Madrid.

The company employed one doctor, the entire medical facility for the town without hospital or nurses. Every man paid a dollar a month for any medical care he might need. When his wife had a baby he paid extra for the delivery. The town's water supply was a sometime thing. Railroad tank cars brought water from springs five miles away, siphoning it into a reservoir. Sometimes the supply became exhausted and pipes were dry for a whole day until another tank came in. Mrs. Lloyd wrote, "Dishes, laundry and baths just had to wait. If you got too thirsty the tavern wasn't too far away."

Electricity was unavailable for homes in 1913. Generated in a powerhouse the current was sufficient only for company houses. Families had to rely on kerosene lamps and candles. Cooking was done on coal fires, the fuel bought "reasonably" from the company. Sometimes a dynamite cap lost in the coal would liven things up in the stove.

CHRISTMAS CITY of New Mexico. Below are most of the buildings remaining in Madrid, all vacant. On hill at right still stands cross that centered electrically lit "replica" of Bethlehem with large cut-outs representing Biblical figures, display one of many completely surrounding town. Surmounting each of 12 hills on both sides of Madrid was huge Christmas "tree"—pine pole with iron bars for limbs, each generously strung with colored light bulbs. Tree in foreground alone remains erect.

Fire was always a hazard, some houses burned through the use of lamps and candles, the company finally wiring them for electricity but limiting them to a single bulb hanging naked from the ceiling, the "juice" turned on only at a given time after nightfall. In time daytime electricity was allowed, for ironing—one day a week.

The men made their living at the company mines and were expected to spend it in the company store. But the drygoods section offered little more than jumpers, overalls and a few women's house dresses. When wives ordered more frilly items from mail-order houses, they had to do it secretly and hope no company official would see her carrying the package home.

All this was before Oscar Huber. He changed everything, literally brought light to shine on Madrid. He became superintendent after working there for several years, bringing his wife and children from Albuquerque. Marjorie Lloyd says of him, "I used to enjoy watching him stride up the street each morning. You sensed in his quick decisive step that he was definitely going some place." Huber planted flower beds in his yard, the only

ones in town, and soon had a showplace, with flower boxes under the windows. When others admired the effect, he made available water flowing from one of the mine tunnels, piping a convenient supply to each section of houses. That summer there were splashes of color in almost every yard.

Huber had the main street paved and new houses built in all lots made vacant by fires. Then came a six-room hospital, first grade and high schools to replace old residences used by students. An employees' club was organized, baseball diamond and bleachers built, Madrid becoming famous for its ball team, the company paying its transportation to compete in other towns. Yet no change in the gloomy, soot-blackened town was as spectacular as allowing all residents unlimited use of electricity.

In the first winter after this innovation, Huber helped the people put on a Christmas display, the like of which had never been seen in New Mexico. Huge figures were created—of Mary, Joseph, the infant Christ, shepherds and wise men. Miners enthusiastically painted and wired them for electrical illumination. The nativity scene, utilizing

OLD CEMETERY on hill above Madrid contains many markers and enclosures individually hand-crafted from local materials. Not all graves are fenced, or wooden pickets have disappeared, many graves marked only by piles of stones.

CACTI "ask but little here below," growing happily on dirt roof of stone house. Plastered inside with mud, it is one of the oldest relics in Madrid, dating from days before large companies took over coal production.

COMPANY HOUSES—4 long lines of nearly identical units—presented dreary sight to residents but now of interest as ghost town relics. Originally standing in Kansas, houses were sawed in quarters, shipped to Madrid on Santa Fe Railroad. Reassembled they were plastered to make windproof but storms soon seeped through. Most had living room, kitchen on main floor, 3 bedrooms upstairs. Danger of fires was always present from overturned kerosene lamps or candles. In absence of water firemen dynamited burning buildings to prevent spread of flames.

live sheep, burros and oxen was set up on a hill overlooking the town, followed by a Bethlehem scene with central cross and many buildings. As each Christmas came, new ones were added until in a few years both sides of the canyon were covered with brilliantly lighted Biblical scenes. Every building in town displayed strings of colored lights and in the ball park was a display for children featuring Santa Claus and mechanically lighted toyland figures.

The magnificent pageant drew thousands of visitors from other parts of the state, the show of lights maintained from early December through New Years. The program set in motion by Oscar Huber gave the miners initiative to organize choral clubs with many fine voices and during evenings of Christmas week various groups were stationed at strategic points, breaking into coordinated song with the words "Let There Be Light." At that instant the main switch was thrown on and the dark old coal town broke into a blaze of glory and glad voices.

In the '30s the town that shipped millions of tons of coal annually began to show signs of slowing down. Gradual conversion in railroading and industry to other fuels slackened coal production.

OLD BEDSTEAD and climbing vine offer composition on wall of old Madrid house.

COMPANY OFFICES near north end of city on road to Los Cerrillos and Santa Fe. Close inspection reveals strings of lights still clinging to structure.

World War II brought it up some temporarily, 20,000 tons going to Los Alamos to help build the first A-bombs. But Madrid's Christmas lights were turned on for the last time in 1941. When the switch was thrown off at the end, the choraleers sang "Auld Lang Syne" while almost everyone wept openly.

GHOSTS ON THE CREST

Golden, New Mexico

The confirmed "shunpiker" could hardly pick a more rewarding route between Albuquerque and Santa Fe than paved New Mexico State 10. Beginning a few miles east of Albuquerque the road spans a short stretch that leads to highly scenic Sandia Crest, 10,678 feet high, and a chain of some of the most picturesque ghost towns in the state. Here were scenes of successive boom and bust in the frantic search for gold, silver, lead, turquoise and more plebian coal.

The first community reached after turning north from U.S. 66 is San Antonitos, an old village populated mostly by Mexican woodcutters and cattle ranchers. Then comes the ancient site of Paako and gold mining camp of San Pedro where only the old coke ovens remain and these hard to find. After that Golden, the only one now visible of what was a cluster of placer camps.

Adjoining Golden at the north was the earlier town of Tuerto ("one-eyed man," in Spanish) where a boom took place in 1839, ten years before the big one in the California Sierra. But there was an older camp just east, around the shoulder of the cluster of peaks called Ortiz Mountains, 8,928 feet. The city editor of the Albuquerque *Tribune* and writer for *New Mexico Magazine*, Ralph Looney, did much research on the old camps in this area. He reports the fact that Dolores, also called Placitas Viejas ("old placers"), was the scene of the first gold rush in what is now the United States. By way of distinguishing it from the more recent camp nearby, it was at first called Placitas Nuevas and was large enough to support twenty-two stores. Both have utterly vanished and Golden is fast decaying.

When placer gold was exhausted in Lazarus Gulch and Tuerto Creek, miners gradually shifted south, deserting Tuerto and forming Golden, where an old church stood, constructed in the early 1830s. In recent years the structure was restored yet it retains the soft adobe lines of the original (see *Tales the Western Tombstones Tell*). The lady tending the little store in 1966 was quite resentful when visitors called the place a "ghost town" but was quite willing to accept their money. As in all near-abandoned towns considerable vandalism has been perpetrated on buildings and cemetery, but this writer believes those who visit any old town because of its historical interest are not the ones who tear up floors to look for treasure or who smash tombstones. Deliberate destruction is more likely to be the work of casual joy-riders out for a thrill or two, their signatures a scattering of empty liquor bottles and beer cans.

VERY OLD STRUCTURES such as this attest age of Golden. Construction here is primitive, using local materials.

TWO BOOMLETS FAILED

San Pedro, New Mexico

Just south of the mining camp of San Pedro are the ruins of an ancient Indian village called Paako, the language spoken there either Keres or Tewa. In 1598 the explorer Onate called the pueblo Tano. The houses were built of native rubble and generally two stories high. There were three kivas, those circular holes in the ground, paved with rock and used as places of worship. Early historians state the pueblo was still occupied as late as 1626 but by 1670 all Indian inhabitants had vanished.

With Spanish occupation a mission was established on the site in 1661 and named San Pedro de la Cuchilla after the patron saint. The University of New Mexico did some excavation at the site in 1936, uncovering traces of stone walls and kivas. Adjoining the remains on the north was the early mining camp also called San Pedro as was the huge Spanish land grant including Indian ruins, mission church and hundreds of acres of pasture land.

The exact date of gold discoveries at San Pedro camp is uncertain but in 1846 army Lt. J. W. Abert visited there. In his report to Congress he said, "In the evening we visited a town at the base of the principal mountains here, mingled with the houses were huge mounds of earth thrown out of the wells so that the village looks like a village of giant prairie dogs. Nearly all of the people were at their wells, and were drawing up bags of loose sand by means of windlasses. Around the pools men, women and children were grouped, intently pouring over their bags of loose sand, washing the earth in wooden platters or goat horns. . . ."

The fevered days of washing and panning by hand did not last long because particles of gold had to be a little larger than "dust" to be discovered in sediments, specks smaller than flakes of coarse pepper usually going undiscovered. Also water had to be available where the gold was. Primitive hand panning was replaced in 1880 by big time hydraulic operations when the San Pedro and Canyon del Agua Company set up equipment. Overlooking the area is the now famed tourist attraction, Sandia Crest. Up there the company found ample water with a steep drop down to San Pedro.

Officials spent $500,000 for a pipeline to carry it into monitors or hydraulic nozzles that would wash whole hillsides into waiting sluices. While the pipeline was being constructed, the company made real estate hay by laying out a town for sales to credulous buyers who were told there would be a big city here. Then the company was beset by extensive litigation, pipeline and town building held up in the courts. Construction became so entangled the company was forced to quit. Again quiet settled over the San Pedro foothills.

A few years later another company moved in, putting up buildings on empty lots and in 1887 the *Golden Nine* was so optimistic as to proclaim, "Everybody is coming to San Pedro and the rest of the world will be used for pasturage," . . . "Newcomers should bring a tent. There are no vacant houses here, there are families living even in the coke ovens. . . ." But that boom died too. There were more recent spurts of activity, for a time during World War I some copper being taken out, but no big time mining has been done for years.

STONE COKE OVENS are only remaining tangible evidence of once roaring gold camp. Coal was hauled by ox team from Madrid to the north, roasted in ovens to drive off easily removed soot, smoke, leaving residue of highly efficient fuel for smelter. With roof already collapsed even this relic will soon become a mere pile of rubble.

SOME ADOBE HOUSES in Lajitas were repaired, covered with new tin roofs during small uranium boom, others exposed to infrequent but heavy downpours, are already melting away. Adobe bricks vary from place to place in binders, extenders, but all have two common characteristics: basic material is native clay and bricks are unfired except by sun. Usually mixed with clay are stones (as here), chopped straw, weeds. These hoed into mixture with water, packed into wooden forms much larger than fired-brick shapes. Partial drying shrinks adobe enough to allow removal of form for further "baking." Adobe building stands solidly as long as roof is intact, walls weathering in rain only slightly. Once roof goes entire building melts rapidly away.

TEXAS

MARFA · ALPINE

SHAFTER

PRESIDIO

OJINAGA

TERLINGUA · STUDY BUTTE

LAJITAS

MEXICO

Texas

A BANDIT LIVENED IT UP

Lajitas, Texas

He was said to be a peaceful lad until he killed an official who raped his sister. Then the teenager Arango took another name and started a career of banditry and revolution. He made many raids on the Texas side of the border, some of them from the easy crossing at Lajitas, and set the state on edge, the army on point. This was Mexico's colorful bandit, Doroteo Aranga, better known as Francisco (Pancho) Villa.

It was naturally, before Pancho Villa, a peaceful village, lying on the Rio Grande River where it flows tranquilly in shallow reaches over easily crossed sand bars just before it plunges into the spectacular Santa Elena Canyon. Aborigines traveling the old Comanche War Trail stopped to rest or camp here overnight, water not being so readily available for many miles farther on. Perhaps some stayed longer, built adobe houses and planted gardens. Vegetables thrived in this region of mild winters, warm summers and plenty of water from the river. Spanish and Anglo explorers found Lajitas (meaning "little flagstones") a village of Indian and Mexican farmers and goat herders drowsing peacefully on the banks of the Rio Grande.

Although on a dirt road Lajitas was a port of entry and the United States took the precaution of sending army troops to protect the rich mining camps of the Big Bend area, by far the largest being Shafter and Lajitas. Gen. John J. Pershing and Lt. Gen. George Patton were there, their tenure

just before the advent of World War I. Villa was murdered in July of 1923, his death ending a period of prosperity of sorts for Lajitas.

It sprang to some activity as the main importation point of a plant growing in abundance on the Mexican side, useful in the manufacture of chewing gum. Locally called "candelia cactus," it was the source of a wax which supplied 45% of Wrigley's

CRACKED, FALLING PLASTER makes pattern on old adobe wall. Finishing plaster coating is simple mud, water mix, smoothed on and often whitewashed. Area in upper left of photo shows detail of brick and same-material mortar construction.

NEAR LAJITAS, Rio Grande, having picked up strength from inflowing Mexican rivers, Rio Conchos and San Carlos, plunges into tremendous slot slashing in two Mesa Anguila range. This view shows top of cut, canyon walls towering 1,500' above stream. Santa Elena Canyon, when entered by intrepid boatmen, holds craft on turbulent, narrowed flood for 8 miles to exit. Several lives have been thus lost but adventurers on modern rubber rafts make exciting trip safely with necks stiff from gazing upward. After short respite river enters Mariscal and Boquillas Canyons before long near-level sweep to Gulf. Top of Santa Elena's rocky gorge seems barren in photo but closer examination reveals wealth of low Sonoran Desert flora. Fascinating variety of cacti and succulents flourish. "Sticks" are last year's and lower stems of agave.

Upper end of Santa Elena Canyon where Rio Grande enters—Mexico on left, Texas right. (Photo Texas State Highway Dept.)

RIO GRANDE, famed in song and story, is Rio Bravo del Norte of Spanish explorers from south. River heads in Colorado's San Juan Mountains forming Continental Divide, flows 1,885 miles to empty 3½ million acre feet of water into Gulf of Mexico yearly, varies from crystal clear in Colorado and Northern New Mexico to famous turbidity of lower reaches between Texas and Mexico. Here stream flows placidly in period of low water, near shore Texas, U.S.A., opposite flood plain and mountains in Chihuahua, Mex. Point of view is between Presidio and Lajitas, Texas.

NATURE WRITER Donald Culross Peattie once said of those easterners who starved in western deserts, "These courageous greenhorns, these corn and beef fed farmers, these small townsmen whose food came out of barrels, sacks and boxes—how could they guess that the Lord had appointed any manna in the valley and shadow of death?"
Peattie was referring specifically to Bennet-Manley party in desperate circumstances, lost in Death Valley in 1849, but point could apply to thousands of pioneers who went hungry while succulent, sweet and nourishing pods of Mesquite bushes hung over their heads. "Mesquite" comes from Nahuatl Indian **mizquitl**, most common species in southwest **Prosopis juliflora.**
Bean pods of plant growing as shrub or small tree can be eaten in green state or ripe seeds can be ground into flour. Roots hold soil, trunk makes good fuel, fence posts, blossoms making excellent honey. Against these are vicious thorns, aggressive takeover of forage lands. Thorn shown here, upper left, explains why careless treatment of thicket is likely to draw blood.

need. Actually a relative of the Christmas time poinsettia and properly *Euphorbia antisyphilitica*, the plant has slender, rodlike branches about three feet high, almost leafless and growing vertically. Around 1949 there was a big boom in candelia but it ended when Mexico placed a ban of exportation of it.

Then came the atom bomb and the frantic search for uranium. Believing a fortune could be found in the Big Bend country, prospectors bought their supplies in Lajitas. The climate tended to dry their throats so the bistros there flourished. With dreams of uranium fortunes fading, the prospectors drifted away and Lajitas was quiet again.

The near ghost town is situated in Brewster County, largest in Texas and one of the most thinly populated. The community was without electricity until 1964 when all of fifteen meters were put into service. Lajitas has the reputation of being several degrees hotter than Presidio which often reports the highest summer temperatures in the United States. Spring, fall and winter months are the best time to explore the Big Bend country, preferably February to June. Even in summer months many high-elevation foot-and-horse trails in the Chisos offer cool comfort.

SILVER IN BANDIT COUNTRY

Shafter, Texas

The sun was good to John Spencer. He probably cursed the glaring, dazzling spot in the sky all day as its heat burned into his back and bounced up from the stony cover to blind him. Water was little solace as it disappeared so fast and his thoughts dwelt so bitterly on the damn foolishness of a Rio Grande rancher to go prospecting when he ought to go to town and get food for his kitchen. He was just about to quit and go back to camp when he saw, glinting in the dusty shafts of the near-setting sun, a shiny streak in a rock. It was nearly pure silver.

He looked around and found other pieces of float, deciding he had surely enough located a projecting lead of silver. Pocketing the sample he strolled back to his camp where "tame" Apaches were preparing supper, saying nothing of his find. The party got an early start for Fort Davis where Spencer purchased his supplies.

Some historians say John Spencer was one of the "original settlers" in the area but there is proof of white men being in that part of Texas in 1571. While some of these first Spaniards were "explorers," some remained to live along the Rio Grande, then called Rio Bravo del Norte. And before that

SEVERAL FAMILIES still live in few adobe cottages remaining more or less intact. Senora Lupe Munoz is lady alcalde of old mining camp, operating store, only business here. She attends to twice daily mail call at post office a block away. Spanish is prevailing language in village, only few of about 20 residents understanding English. Rocky foothills of Chinati Mts. seem entirely barren but support wealth of plants appearing exotic to northern strangers—many kinds of agaves, more cacti species than most southwest sections.

an advanced Indian civilization flourished there as long ago as 8,000 B.C.

Until Fort Davis was established in 1854, Milton Faver was the only Anglo-American to settle in the Big Bend country. Fluent in several languages, Faver was thought to have fatally wounded a man in one of the southern states and escaping to Mexico, joined a cattle train traveling north on the very long established Chihuahua trail. Crossing the Rio Grande at Ojinaga he dropped out to set up a ranch-fort at a point later called Cibolo. At that time the water table was much higher than now, creeks flowing abundantly and steadily to make a lush growth of grass. Faver ran cattle on his ranch and later at other nearby locations, Cienaga and El Morita. It was generally supposed to be impossible for a white man to hold out against marauding Apaches for any length of time but Faver did and others were encouraged to follow. Some lost their lives in Indian attacks but one who lived to thrive was John Spencer, his ranch a few miles from Cibolo as was the place of his silver find.

Adjacent to the military establishment of Fort Davis was the little town of the same name. As Spencer suspected, the assay office there reported

OLD SHAFTER CEMETERY lacks softening influence of green grass, shrubs, trees, is typical of burial grounds in arid sections. Area at right rear is "populated" by descendants of earliest settler Milton Faver. He died in 1890s, is buried on his Cibolo ranch, now inaccessible. His son Juan had daughter Francisca who married Ira Cline and still lives at Shafter, giving this reporter much of mining town story. "Many victims of mine accidents rest under those stones in cemetery," she said in Spanish. Identifying descriptions on wooden crosses are completely weathered away.

his sample to be heavily laden with silver but he kept his secret well. He was not known as a prospector, simply a rancher laying food supplies.

At the time there was an outburst of the always smouldering hatred between the original dwellers on the land encompassed by the Big Bend of the Rio Grande and the white settlers. Ranches were pillaged, buildings burned, women carried off. Could Spencer, in the face of widely scattered attacks, safely start and carry on a mining operation? To make sure he could Spencer shared his secret with Major Shafter, in charge of cavalry, and Indian fighter Lt. John L. Bullis.

Major Shafter, later made full general, must have been something of a financial genius. In San Francisco he raised enough capital to start the Presidio Mining Co., then joined his cavalry with the Seminole-Negro scouts of Lt. Bullis. Although the Chinati Mountains were teeming with lurking Apaches they had little chance against a concerted attack by trained soldiers and were soon all killed or put in full retreat. That left the field clear to start mining.

Everything needed for it was hard to come by being so far away from source of supplies. Machinery was at first shipped from the east by Southern Pacific to the rail crossing of the ancient Chihuahua Trail, thence to camp by freight wagon and assembled at the mill site on Cibolo Creek where there was an ample water supply. Furnace fuel was delivered on contract by a wood-cutting firm which stripped the fine oak and sycamore groves along water courses and pines from high elevations—which have never regrown due to lack of water.

Mexicans from both sides of the border nearby were employed as laborers, most of them honest and reliable. One who was not caused a small scale riot in Shafter a few years after the town was started. Always a drinker, he spent a good share of his payday dollars in one of the several cantinas and then declared he wanted a woman. Si, si—he

RUINED BUILDING is near mill site, was likely residence or office of mine, mill officials. Photo shows structure in brilliant, head-on morning sunshine. Accompanying photo shows building in late afternoon light with near-setting making star pattern in door opening.

could have one of those handy at the *burdel* on a back street but he wanted class. On the main pike he openly propositioned every senora and senorita he met and then attempted to rape a girl in the middle of the street. Free and easy citizens thought this edging beyond good reason and had the local constabulary grab the miscreant and tie him to a tree until he could be taken to the nearest jail, in Marfa.

During the night several miners untied the man, took him out of town and shot him to death. Fearing further trouble the company called in the Texas Rangers. The famous early law men arrived, quieted all outward signs of violence and departed without the actual culprits being identified. At a dance held soon afterward a quarrel broke out between those who sympathized with the lynch mob and those who favored the law. Gunfire and stabbings caused authorities to call the Rangers back which neither faction liked as they felt they could settle their own squabbles. Joining forces all gathered in a barricaded building and when the Rangers approached they were met by a blast of rifle fire which killed one and wounded several. The Rangers returned some fire, inflicting casualties on the rebels inside and held them trapped. Reinforcements arrived and they surrendered, allowed to return to their jobs after a short cooling off period.

All wood supplies for mill furnaces were exhausted by 1910 but oil was then available and hauled in by truck from Marfa. Mine shafts penetrated the limestone to pockets of silver at depths of 700 feet. Writing for *True West*, Robert Graham says some of the silver concentrations yielded as much as $500 per ton of ore. By 1913 mules used to haul ore from mine to mill were replaced by tram and in 1914 came the exciting period of the Mexican Revolution and Pancho Villa.

Villa, deeply involved in the revolution that deposed dictator Don Porfirio Diaz and installed as president Francisco Madero, retired on funds supplied by Madero. He went to live in Juarez, El Paso on this side of the border not offering the luxuries he wanted, but leisure was not Villa's "kind of country." When President Madero was assassinated by Don Victoriano Huerta, Villa planned a coup against Huerta. He had friends in Ojinaga, Mexico, but could not go there safely with Huerta in power, so he looped around by way of El Paso, Valentine and Shafter. He rested at the mining camp and went on to the border, marshalling willing forces at Ojinaga.

At once Villa set out to attack his bitter enemy Gen. Orozco who had once sentenced the bandit to death for horse stealing, a fate escaped through help from Madero. Orozco and forces were routed, fleeing into Texas, a flagrant violation of neutrality laws. According to common rumors he knew the area around Shafter, had in 1913 escorted Gen. Luiz Tarrazas to an abandoned mine shaft there to conceal a fortune in gold and silver the absconding general had spirited across the Rio Grande. And this time Orozco was carrying some $80,000 in bills of large denomination.

Encountering a party of Americans he exchanged gunfire with them, hurriedly buried his loot somewhere on Eagle Mountain and slipped into Shafter to hide out with old friends. According to the tale once the heat was off, Orozco retrieved his fortune and added it to the hoard in the mine tunnel. Then he recrossed the Rio Grande, hoping to return eventually and secure his treasure to live the life of leisure in Mexico. What he had not counted on was the implacable hatred of Pancho Villa who was hot on his trail. He died while still running from the bandit without revealing the location of his cache of riches.

At its peak operation there were 4,000 people in Shafter, 500 men in the silver mines, prosperity for town and company lasting until 1931 when the price of silver dropped to 25c an ounce which brought mining to a grinding halt. During Pres. Roosevelt's time silver values rose to reactivate it.

In WPA days Shafter was said to have a population of 300. "It is a far cry," says the Texas Writers' Program, *Guide to the Lone Star State*, "from urban luxuries to this village of adobe houses tucked away in this mountain wilderness. Hidden trails to the south are still frequented by smugglers and raids by Mexican bandits occur. Life is often lonely for officials of the mines. Free barbecues are a favorite pastime, but owing to the difficulty at times of freighting in sufficient refreshments for the guests, invitations for such festivities have borne the initials B.Y.O.B. (bring your own beer)." This level of activity lasted until 1942 when mines were again closed, this time the machinery removed which seemed to ring the death knell.

But in 1954 the few people left in town were thrilled to see surveyors and prospectors employed by Anaconda Lead and Silver Co. working in town and the surrounding Chinatis. Rumors circulated that the firm would resume mine operations, that ore would be hauled to Marfa for refining since no water existed in Cibolo Creek except in unpredictable floods. Anaconda said only that its men had located vast reserves of high grade lead and silver in the Chinatis, but their men went away and never came back.

Today Shafter is very quiet industrially. There is no grind of tramway cables or noise of revolving ball mills, and there are no Mexican mine workers singing ballads in their homes in the evening. Yet an inspiring medley of sounds does reward the ghost town scout who camps overnight in some thicket of mesquite trees on a deserted back street. Morning brings cascading bird songs and calls unequalled in the west. Chirps, trills and cadenzas are linked together by the varied overtones of mocking birds, more numerous than any other. Not too intrusive is an occasional challenging rooster crow from the yard of one of the ten families remaining to remember a lively past.

ARID SOUTHWEST AREA generally is lacking in timber. Early builders here erected structures of material available, the earth underfoot. Clay was mixed with water, often combined with straw, weeds or other binder, then shaped into large bricks and laid in hot sun to dry. Walls made of adobe blocks were almost proof against heat and cold, but vulnerable to rain, lasting until protection of roof failed, then slowly succumbing to weather.

TYPICAL RUINS display both stone and adobe construction. Holes at top of adobe wall once held beams, **vigas**, supporting brush and mud roof. Grass, hay or weeds were used in most adobe bricks, weathered-out samples evident in those at lower right. Holes at upper edge seem to have been made by rifle bullets.

THREE TONGUES — THREE TOWNS

Terlingua, Texas

Old Terlingua was situated at the junction of 50 mile long Terlingua Creek and the Rio Grande. When the first Spanish speaking travelers arrived there well before 1800 they found a village of adobe huts and corrals built of spiny ocotillo canes. The natives were peaceable Indians but savage Apache tribes attacked at intervals, driving out both Mexicans and Indians. The natives invariably returned to find homes destroyed, domestic animals driven off or killed for food.

About 1859 a troop of U.S. Cavalry arrived with supplies on backs of mules and camels. They did not remain permanently but the threat of unex-

pected return had a restraining influence on the raiders. Yet the menace of them was not removed until 1880. The name Terlingua almost certainly corrupted from the Spanish *tres lenguas* but what were they, the three languages? Originally the name referred to a tiny Indian village on the banks of the Rio Grande just above its plunge into the narrow-walled Santa Elena Canyon. Early Spanish explorers are said to have found the Indian inhabitants of Terlingua speaking three distinct idioms. Another theory is that after some Spanish and later Americans settled in the area, the three languages were Indian, Spanish and English.

When cinnabar was discovered in the hills just

IMPOSING MANSION on hill was placed to allow superintendent's observation of entire town and mine workings. Built by owner Howard Perry but not used continuously by him. He spent most of his time in Chicago after Terlingua mines were well established. Smaller adjoining structure at far right served first as stable, later as garage.
During period when Pancho Villa was raiding border towns, Perry made hurried visit to Terlingua, ordered superintendent to sandbag and barricade parapets of house, keep guards posted with order to fire on any suspicious strangers. "Constable" Bob Cartledge soothed excited owner, argued that constant presence of U.S. troops not far away would be enough protection.

LONG, BRICK-PAVED CORRIDOR follows entire east length of house. View here to southeast shows old store framed in second arch from left. Barren Hills at rear are still in Texas, those at extreme right part of Sierra Mulato, Chihuahua, Mexico. Mansion has no inner hallway, all offices and first floor rooms opening on walk. Each has fireplace and wall-recessed shrine.

above the old village, the town growing up around the mines was also called Terlingua, or Terlingua-Chisos, the name of the largest and oldest mine. In further complication, when these mines were flooded out underground in 1942, what was left of operations went near the still-producing Mariposa mine, a post office named Terlingua established there. So there were three towns of the name too.

Just who found the first cinnabar in the area? There is no record but a modest amount of the brilliant red, softish, mercury-yielding rock was mined around old Terlingua. The cattle wranglers, Devine McKinney and Jess Parker, who accidentally found a red outcropping while rounding up some stray cows were not aware of its potential value. They secured the cows and went back to do enough digging to believe the deposit was extensive and perhaps worth claiming.

Discreet inquiry revealed the property had recently been acquired by a man completely unknown in the area, Howard E. Perry. McKinney and Parker learned he was in the lumber business in Portland, Maine, and wrote to ask if he would sell his Texas property. Not hearing for several months they wrote again and still heard nothing.

There was a reason. Perry was thinking. Described by Texas historian Ed Syers as "tight-fisted, close-mouthed," he suspected a reason behind the unusual interest and hired lawyer Wingfall Van Sickle of Alpine, 90 miles distant, to get the facts. Van Sickle rode a horse to the Indian village, pronounced the reason as cinnabar and by urgent message advised Perry to secure title to the property firmly and start mining. Perry heeded the advice, went to Terlingua, set up full scale operations and hired experienced Robert Lee Cartledge of Austin to manage the property.

The quicksilver operations started under extremely primitive conditions. All equipment was hauled the 90 miles from Alpine over a sandy trail in the river washes, wagons of the old Studebaker freighting type hauled by twelve Spanish mules used to profanity. And the finished product, mercury, was shipped north by the same means.

While sometimes found in the pure state the metal is almost always combined with sulphur to form cinnabar, mercuric sulphide. The Terlingua area ore is brilliant vermilion, soft enough to rub off on the hands and for use by Indians as war paint. Piles of ore, ready to be roasted for separation of quicksilver, still stand near the old Rainbow mine at Study Butte near Terlingua, appearing like heaps of glowing coals in the hot sunshine.

Terlingua was always plagued by water trouble—too little above ground, too much in the lower levels of the mines. For a long time a tiny spring was piped downhill to a town tank, the precious liquid rationed at two pailsful per day per family. These were carried uphill by shoulder yoke to some tiny tin-roof adobe or ocotillo cane, mud-plastered shack. Or if the family owned a burro a carreta could be hauled to the Rio Grande for a full cask of that kind of water. Most of the time it was as said, "Too thick to drink, too thin to plow." Later, when ground water became a menace to the mines,

HEADFRAME in background. Built of bolted 12x12s, structure supported cable system operating two cages allowing continuous up and down traffic. Shaft drops 600', laterals at 50' intervals. Horizontal tunnels, interlacing, connecting total 50 miles in length, some reaching under old cemetery where miners killed in accidents were buried. At left background is waste dump, comparatively small due to richness of Terlingua ore. Rock houses, now roofless, were homes of better-paid miners, some officials. Ordinary laborers lived in tin or adobe shacks.

it was pumped out for the mills and domestic use.

The town was strictly company owned, right down to the little jail with iron rings in the floor. An industrious Mexican laborer could earn up to $2 a day and whether he spent it for food at the company store or tequilla at the company cantina, Howard Perry got it in the end. If an over-thirsty peon got drunk and was thrown in the company's own *carcel*, he could bail out with a fine. The company "court" got this too.

Ed Syers, author of *Off the Beaten Trail*, asked Bob Cartledge, retired in Austin, about the jail's leg irons. "We didn't use them," Cartledge said. "Just the sentence, 'report to jail on Saturday!' If he had a sick wife he could come when convenient." "Constable" Cartledge may possibly have forgotten

a few disagreeable incidents in Terlingua's history. The rings in the floor show signs of some use.

Perry's Chisos and Terlingua Mining Companies hardly paid their way at first. The demand for mercury fluctuates to an extreme. Gold discoveries in California in the late 1840s and '50s created a sudden need for the liquid metal used in gold amalgamation, mercury later driven off as steam, cooled and saved. At that time the only source was Spain, shipping a near impossibility. Luckily cinnabar was found in California at just the right time. In Terlingua the demand for mercury was moderate over the years, prices generally low, until World War I started when the demand boosted the town's economy to the point where $2,000

SEVERE BUILDING, strictly utilitarian, served as assay offices where steady stream of core samples drilled from deep-down bedrock were analyzed. Fading or expanding values in cores controlled direction of penetration in rock. Short distance from photographer is yawning shaft opening, many hundreds of feet deep, no head structure or barricade to warn of danger. In background is rear of officers' quarters.

REFINERY MILL, one of several almost open to the sky. Cinnabar, mercury ore, composed of metal combined with various sulphur compounds, was roasted for separation. While both mercury and sulphur are volatile, latter vaporizes first, is driven off without opportunity to cool, solidify. Quicksilver follows at slightly higher temperatures, (357°C - 675°F) is vapor-cooled and condensed into normal liquid form.

Finished mercury, named for speedy Greek god, was packaged in "flasks", steel cylinders. Threaded at one end, when filled they were sealed tight by steel screw-in plug. Fit must be perfect, quicksilver making way through tiniest opening, as hairlike tube in thermometer, and no sealing compound could be used for stopper because of danger of contaminating product. Flask weighed fraction over 76 pounds, equalling weight of pottery containers Romans used for mercury. They called heft **quintal,** 100 libre. Quart of heavy liquid would weigh 28 pounds.

was rolling in every day. These were Terlingua's golden years.

During this period the Chisos Company greatly expanded all facilities including the store. A six-pew church was built, brick factory, large hotel, several cafes, even an adobe movie house. Local baseball and basketball teams were said to equal all rivals in the area. About this time a company of infantry in the Texas State Guard, says Texas historian Dick King, was made up entirely of Terlingua men.

The decline that followed the end of the war brought panic to Terlingua. Perry over-extended his Chisos operations in a desperate attempt to maintain war-time prosperity, and lost all he owned. The property stood idle for a few years and some families remained in hope things would

pick up, most of these gradually moving away to leave but a half dozen houses occupied. In 1946 all residents were ordered out, homes dismantled and all valuable mill machinery removed, Terlingua becoming a deserted city.

Today it is a fascinating ghost, completely deserted except for a caretaker at the old store making welcome the few visitors who reach this remote area. A sign, posted conspicuously near the open gate, warns sternly of open, dangerous shafts. The warning is not over-emphasized. Everywhere there are yawning holes where a person could drop hundreds of feet. Running children and pets should be confined to the car. Summers are likely to be hot, with temperatures often highest in the nation, but a dry atmosphere relieves oppression.

SIMMERING in one of U.S. hottest spots are ruins of adobe buildings that housed company offices at Study Butte. With protective coating of plaster gone historic building is not long for this world.

ADJACENT TO OLD HOSTELRY were stables, "parking places" for wagons. Study Butte has had minimum amount of vandalism, possibly because old store was more or less continuously occupied.

GENERAL VIEW of Study Butte shows company offices in foreground, stables in middle distance left, still operating store near center. Fringes of hills, mountains in background, lie across Rio Grande in Mexico. Photo was sent author by Texas State Highway Dept. with information, "Considerable activity has recently been noted at Study Butte, but information as to nature is unavailable and property is now posted. Assumption is that quicksilver mining will be resumed soon."